LIVING
Your Destiny

LIVING
Your Destiny

———by———
Hal A. Lingerman

SAMUEL WEISER, INC.

York Beach, Maine

First published in 1992 by
Samuel Weiser, Inc.
Box 612
York Beach, ME 03910

Library of Congress Cataloging-in-Publication Data

Lingerman, Hal A., 1943–
    Living your destiny / Hal A. Lingerman.
        p.   cm.
    Includes bibliographical references.
        1. Symbolism of numbers. 2. Self-realization
(Psychology)--Miscellanea. 3. Vital Force--Miscellanea.
4. Pythagoras and Pythagorean school—Miscellanea. I.
Title.
BF1623.P9L57   1992
133.3'35 – dc20   92-7903
                                                       CIP

ISBN 0-87728-746-5
BJ

Cover art © 1992 Jonathan Wiltshire. Used by kind permission of the artist.

Printed in the United States of America

The paper used in this publication meets the minimum
requirements of the American National Standard for Per-
manence of Paper for Printed Library Materials
Z39.48-1984.

Table of Contents

How much nicer it is to vibrate to a large number of frequencies; how sad it would be to tune in only to yourself. . . . The character of all things, in a sense, is determined by what they respond to. . . . In truth, the larger patterns of getting in and out of tune with various things and persons are often more rich and lasting than any single tune itself.

—*K.C. Cole*

So teach us to number our days, that we may apply our hearts unto wisdom.

—*Psalm 90:12*

Preface

Are you really living the life you were born to live?
Are you deeply in touch with what truly gives your
life meaning?

Working as a counselor and teacher, it is my privilege to
touch the lives of many people. What I enjoy the most is
sharing with others in their life journey and experiencing
their courage. In the midst of seeking their dreams and
moving through struggles, people often seem to become
aware of definite themes and specific patterns that emerge
for them. Throughout many hours of varied conversations
with others, I have found these two questions most frequently surfacing:

1. What do I *really* want in my life?

2. What am I here to learn, for what was I born?

Each life is ultimately a mystery, revealing its own unique,
unfolding processes; each life contains its own particular
material and patterns. This book suggests certain essential, archetypal energies that supply us with the ingredients of our life. Such energies also offer us diverse opportunities and a variety of means to express our deepest
intentions and purposes. As our perspective increases, we
can learn how to make clearer choices. In greater attune-

ment with the energies that surround us, we move in
directions that will enhance the present and future.

In every life there is always the interplay between personal desires, our dreams and hopes, and the way life
leads us, the discovery of our own particular destiny.
What we might like to see happen and what actually *does*
happen are sometimes quite similar, or they may be complementary, or they may remain quite different and far
apart. It seems to me that the most creative lives are those
in which people find ways to integrate their personal
dreams and their destiny: they discover the openings and
rhythms that allow them to achieve a harmonious blending of personal "wants" with what life is requiring of
them.

This book offers an approach to life-mapping: helping
people to gain larger perspectives and a feeling for ways in
which they can express more completely the unique content of their own life path. While certain basic archetypal
patterns exist as processes for everyone to draw upon, all
human beings respond differently, resonating with the
larger energy streams according to their temperament: in
ways prompted by conscious and unconscious leadings.
The journey, therefore, is different and amazingly special
for each person. Likewise, it is the miracle of people interacting with people that often best teaches and empowers
all of us in our diversity. Most important is one's awareness, the integrity of being true to one's own life path. In
this sense, therefore, we can view each other's life and
experiences only with compassion, never with judgmental
eyes.

When we feel in harmony with our desires and awareness, our behaviors become more agreeable and congru-
ent. We feel connected with the way life is moving. It is
then that we may sense a deeper purpose in our existence,
which is not clear when we are living more superficially
and haphazardly. When we feel connected with life, we

may also live more joyfully, receptive to a spontaneity and playfulness in the midst of our activities. Energy increases, and we find a deeper, creative focus. Dr. Bernie Siegel, a sensitive and perceptive physician, has also mentioned many times in his writings and interviews the need to be in harmony with one's life path. It seems that there is a plan, something like a blueprint, that influences our behaviors and emotional responses, as well as our thinking and our spiritual unfoldment. If we are not true or connected to this inner impetus, the distortions in our living eventually become blatantly clear to us, in the form of distress or even disease.

In the spectrum of our creative expression, powerful universal essences of energy open before us, providing us with the archetypes, patterns, issues, and opportunities for our life. All of these energies flow through each of us, animating our total being in varied themes, combinations, and proportions, according to our receptive consciousness and our life experience. As we learn how to contact the great universal life streams of energy that vibrate in our midst, we will overcome dysfunctional tendencies and codependent behaviors. We will experience increasing empowerment and deeper resonance with the great Mystery.

Hal A. Lingerman
Altadena, California, 1992

Acknowledgments

I would like to express my gratitude to the many people I have worked with, professionally and just as one person meeting others on the Path. Especially, I wish to thank Ruth Stockton, friend and first-rate editor, for her expertise and her many valuable suggestions. Finally, I want to acknowledge my wonderful wife and best friend, Rosemary, and my daughter, Aria, who continuously fill my life with magic, uncertainty, love and adventure.

In addition, I would like to credit the following sources for quoted material that appears at the beginning of each section:

K.C. Cole, *Sympathetic Vibrations* (New York: Bantam Books, 1985), pp. 270, 275.

George Oliver, *The Pythagorean Triangle* (Grand Rapids, MI: Wizards Book Shelf, 1975), p. 15, 192–3.

Geoffrey Hodson, *The Hidden Wisdom of the Bible* (Adyar, India: Theosophical Publishing House, 1963), vol. I, p. 148.

Ernest Wilson, *You and the Universe* (San Diego, CA: Harmonial Publishers, 1925), pp. 36–37, 46.

Dorothy Gillam Baker, *Humanity in the Balance of Opposites* (unpublished, 1978), p. 12.

Erik Erikson, *Childhood and Society* (New York: Norton & Co., Inc., 1963), p. 247.

Hildegard of Bingen, quoted in Gabriele Uhllein, *Meditations of Hildegard* (Santa Fe, NM: Bear & Company, 1982), p. 111.

The Kybalion (Chicago: Yogi Publication Society, 1912), p. 149.

W. Wynn Westcott, *Numbers* (London, England: Theosophical Publications, 1973), p. 39.

A. Tory, *Wonder* (New York: Ballantine Publications, 1973), p. xiii.

AE, *Candle of Vision* (Wheaton, IL: Quest Books, 1965), pp. 170, 172.

Mother Teresa, *The Love of Christ* (New York: Harper & Row, 1982), pp. 15, 17. Italics added.

M. Scott Peck, *The Road Less Traveled* (New York: Touchstone, 1978), p. 87.

Jack London, *The Sea Wolf* (Pleasantville, NY: Reader's Digest Assoc. Inc., 1989), p. 123.

Ignace Lepp, *The Ways of Friendship* (New York: MacMillan Co., 1966), pp. 26, 27, 116, 117, 119, 127.

Max Picard, *The World of Silence* (South Bend, IN: Gateway, Inc., 1952), pp. 74, 79.

Teilhard de Chardin, *The Divine Milieu* (New York: Harper & Row, 1957), p. 139.

Douglas V. Steere, *On Being Present Where You Are* (Lebanon, PA: Pendle Hill, 1967), p. 13.

Henry David Thoreau, quoted in Henry Canby, *Thoreau* (Boston: Houghton Mifflin Co.), p. 351.

LIVING
Your Destiny

Introduction

The creation of the world [is] nothing more than the harmonious effect of a pure arrangement of number.

— The Pythagorean School

By the study of numbers, one may learn the fundamental laws of the creation, constitution, and progressive events in the lives of both universes and persons; for man is a modification of cosmic elements, a concentration of cosmic forces.

— Geoffrey Hodson

I believe that we all enter this lifetime to express personal desires and a destiny that are uniquely our own. We are born to be ourselves—in particular ways that life uses us—ways that nobody else can ever duplicate. Already when we are infants, the wheels of fortune greet us, spinning our lives with new rounds and processes, stimulating our responses and choices. Connected to an eternal Radiance, we must yet discover ways to harmonize our particular path and temperament with other lives and the larger, collective earth community. Thus, our lives become a deepening awareness: a growing sense of mystery and purpose, joined together by the common connection with a limitless, resonating, empowering universal love that teaches us how all of life's challenges can be ultimately workable.

Basic universal energies and patterns provide all of us with a common storehouse of challenges that stimulate us to grow into our fullest expression of Divinity in personhood. Different people, meeting various testings, will direct their responses in ways that are resistant or productive. Our energy must find release in some direction: toward well-being or dysfunction. In the description of the particular disorder, lies the solution that unlocks the greater power. The choice is denial and resistance or the process of contact, appreciation, and integration. Receptive to the natural movement of life and to the recesses of our own unconscious, we can learn to modify our attitudes and behaviors; we can free our energy to move in more creative, appropriate directions. Sometimes, what now may seem to be a great loss, disappointment, misfortune or sacrifice is really the beginning of new joy and healing. In this book we can discover ways to keep energy flexible, alert, and diversified; we can learn how better to live our deepest desires and destinies, not our dysfunctions.

Powerful, cosmic sources of energy offer each of us a shining panoply of possibilities and choices. Like a stargazer, viewing the radiant heavens, we can discover more luminous horizons that await the contact of a larger imagination and consciousness. Such horizons and pathways of energy are available to us; they touch the constellations of our temperament, stimulating our awareness through reflection, sudden crises, meditation and prayer, beauty, creativity, joy, a loving relationship or other mysterious processes. Deeper layers of our own unconscious also act as coils of powerful energy that speak to our perception. Unlimited sources of energy surround us, activating our lives.

Pythagoras, the master teacher of ancient Greece, tuned into a larger vision of human potential. He sensed clearly the existence of mighty, universal power streams that feed our lives. These energy streams emanate glistening archetypes and essences that spread like jewels from the heavens, penetrating and inspiring our receptive consciousness. They activate our perception, speak through our own unconscious, and can illumine our choices and responses.

From the scattered writings of Pythagoras, his followers, and others who share his vision, we can identify nine primary energy streams and their thematic content. Taken individually and, more holistically, together, these forces of cosmic power provide ample resources and a clear spectrum for human, creative fulfillment. Because these energy streams are vast and inexhaustible, Pythagoras could not adequately name them. Instead, he simply assigned a number to each of the mighty pathways, as a means of distinguishing the essence of their vibrational themes and movements. Pythagoras realized that "sound, number and color are the three manifestations of the Divine in Nature, Nature's alphabet, so to speak. These three produce a fourth, form."[1] Thus, a certain pathway, called "2," has its own vibration and thematic essences, called TWOness, which differs noticeably from the content of another pathway, such as FIVEness. In this way Pythagoras identified definite energy sources available to all of us. As the esoteric writer, Corinne Heline, sums it up:

---

[1]F. H. & H. Curtiss, *The Voice of Isis* (New York: E.P. Dutton, 1919), p. 358.

The great principles of numbers are focusing points or attracting mediums of high cosmic forces. Without these central transmitting stations, there could be no manifest or visible creation.[2]

This book describes the nine energy pathways, suggested by Pythagoras—the themes and potentials contained within them. Briefly, they can be identified as follows:

1—Individuality and Providence
2—Affiliation and Trusted Partnership
3—Creativity and Imagination
4—Purposefulness and Achievement
5—Life Experience and Sensation
6—Caring for Family, Society and Group
7—Deeper Truth and Knowledge of Mysteries
8—Power and Success
9—Compassion and Brotherhood

These NINE power streams focus energy through the physical, emotional, mental, and intuitive vehicles of every person, thus activating our perceptions and creative responses. A person who may be more strongly connected to certain energy pathways than to others would naturally demonstrate the archetypes and behaviors that are most characteristic of those particular streams. The more totally attuned an individual is to the complete spectrum of the varied power streams, the more expansive and varied is his or her life expression.

By learning how to tune into all the different energy pathways, a person can contact new frequencies of power that speak to the unconscious, as well as to the outer self.

2C. Heline, *The Sacred Science of Numbers* (Los Angeles: New Age Press, 1977), p. 10.

We are thus better able to sense our "blocks" and resistances, and can begin to move toward a larger synthesis and transformation. Recovery and regeneration begin to occur.

Numbers are really symbols for energies that convey to us the deeper nature of structures and processes in the cosmos. For Pythagoras and other sensitive thinkers, numbers are more than just mathematical quantities or literal figures. The science of number is that of living, cosmic energies: number is a realm of Divine Light and Power, which penetrates the earth and all our lives. Number releases energies described in "numbers," a diverse spectrum of creative forces and patterns:

> Numbers announce and broadcast programs of thought, feeling and action being enacted on the television screen of human relations. They are signposts to guide, protect and empower all who have the wisdom and foresight to observe and understand.[3]

In this way numbers represent vast energy conduits, converging in every human being's consciousness and thus forming streams of life activity. In his excellent book, *Avalanche*, Dr. Brugh Joy affirms the powerful symbolism of numbers, as energies, when he says:

> An intuitive perspective can [view] numbers in terms of psychological symbolism. . . . When [numbers] are regarded from psychological and symbolic viewpoints, they can be of immense help in understanding the principal dynamics of life and the human Unconscious.[4]

---

[3]J. Jordan, *Numerology: The Romance of Your Name* (Santa Barbara, CA: J. F. Rowny Press, 1965), p. 7.
[4]B. Joy, *Avalanche* (New York: Ballantine, 1990), p. 164.

Number is the source and root of all things, and in the numbers 1 – 10, we can observe the diversity of multiple manifestations in a unified continuum. Number is, therefore, a universal principle, as real as light (electromagnetism) or sound. As modern physics has demonstrated, it is precisely the numeric, vibrational frequency of electromagnetic energy – the "wavelength" which determines its particular manifestation. Through number we approach the mystery of *logos*: the word of God, issuing from the subtle currents of energy that demonstrate the relation of one to another and all lives to the great Totality.[5] The French writer Balzac calls NUMBER "an Entity and a Breath, emanating from God. . ., the Breath which alone could organize the physical cosmos."[6]

The varied nuances of the great power streams of NUMBERS help us to learn how best to direct our energy: at times we need to focus and concentrate; other situations call for forward direction, like the movement of an arrow; sometimes variety and greater diversification are needed. The plentiful energies of the universe supply us with the needed rhythms and proportions that are most appropriate in a given moment. New, creative integrations and resolutions become continuously possible as we contact more deeply those great universal energy sources, called by number. Such authors as those already mentioned and Hodson, Curtiss, Heline, Newhouse, Wilson, and others have found increasing evidence for these great universal power streams. It is the purpose of this book to provide you with practical, workable approaches to number, which will further release the creative healing powers available to you and all persons. Number contains the empowering energies that help all of us to confront and

---

[5]K. Guthrie, *The Pythagorean Sourcebook and Library* (Grand Rapids, MI: Phanes Press, 1988), p. 21.
[6]F. H. & H. Curtiss, *The Key to the Universe* (New York: E. P. Dutton, 1919), p. 23.

move through the shadows of our unconscious; number invites us to contact and express our greatest hopes and dreams, and suggests to us the mysterious calling of our divine destiny—that is our birthright.

 The
Energy
of
ONEness

The number one represents the glory of God made manifest. . . . The figure 1 - the perpendicular line, is a symbol that suggests the unity between man and God.

—*Ernest Wilson*

The Pioneer [oneness] is often an impulse, an inward necessity to break away from the hold on us of the old, the known, the habitual, the established. . . . There is a need to be free of and to transcend the old order. . . . Life breaks loose . . . in a movement toward something new and unique.

—*Dorothy Gillam Baker*

Keys to ONEness

In the energy of ONEness, certain key themes emerge. You can ask yourself questions that center around the areas of individuality, autonomy, and independent thinking:

1) Do you enjoy leadership positions and trouble-shooting situations?

2) Do you consider yourself to be a good motivator?

3) Are your interests often found in areas of pioneer thinking?

4) In your thinking are you more interested in new possibilities and futuristic ideas?

5) Does your life style offer many new opportunities that require taking risks?

6) Are you easily bored by routine and repetition?

7) In conversation do you get excited by new ideas more than from sharing feelings or talking about familiar topics?

8) In jobs and relationships do you prefer independence, autonomy, and doing your own thing?

9) Do you tend to avoid those who may take issue with your plans and ideas?

10) Are you impatient with those who do not "catch on" quickly?

These questions help connect you with some of the basic energies and patterns of ONEness. If most of your answers were *yes*, you are quite likely strongly attuned to this power stream.

The Energy of ONEness
in World Symbolism

The energy of ONEness describes a center of unity for all vibrations. ONEness emanates the Light of God—a blazing synthesis of all colors blended into the single whiteness of Divine glory and radiance. As an example of the power of ONEness, we can mention Psalm 19, a piece of writing that describes the glory of God made manifest. The energy of ONEness is like a tongue of flame, which kindles the power of the Highest and ignites all creation. Such energy is forceful, "masculine, a fire of divine manifestation in mankind."[1] The energy of ONEness suggests primacy—"the indivisible that is independent of others."[2] The upright position of the symbol, 1, signifies our vertical reach like a rocket exploding toward the heavens and our contact with an all-embracing Infinite Presence. ONEness is a mighty tree trunk, rising up to emerge as a full expression of the great tree of life.

The energy stream of ONEness describes origin and self-sufficiency: one substance, God, from which emanates all life and expression. Aristotle underlines the importance of ONE when he writes about First Cause, the Supreme Form, the Unmoved Mover, that initiates all movement and form for the many: That which is the first of all things is that which imparts motion to all things.[3]

The power of ONEness contains the latent forces of all the energies as they await manifestation in diversity. The energy of ONEness is whole in itself—indivisible. "It is incapable of multiplication."[4] Therefore, it is strongly sym-

---

[1]C. Heline, p. 1.
[2]E. W. Bullinger, *Number in Scripture* (London, England: Lamp Press, 1952), p. 50.
[3]Aristotle, *The Metaphysics*, quoted in Nicholas Capaldi, *Journey Through Philosophy* (Buffalo, NY: Prometheus Books, 1982), p. 128.
[4]R. H. & H. Curtiss, *The Voice of Isis*, p. 62.

bolic of God first or the great primary glory of God. It is an energy that fills the mind in a way that brings wholeness — an idea that enters a person in an undifferentiated state and later emerges in its myriad aspects. ONEness brings audacity, like the heroic, fearless fountain, gushing upward.

In its own individual empowerment, ONEness symbolizes the human being's ability to stand erect: the vertical spinal column and an "uprightness of body, mind and character." Esoterically, the symbol of the silver cord (Ecclesiastes 12:6) describes the power of ONEness — the vital force in us, and the integration of personality and the deeper self which finds its true height in God. The Christ summarized the energy of ONEness when he said, "I and my Father are ONE."

To summarize: the energy of ONEness activates the mind and thinking. Like white light, ONEness carries in itself the latent, dynamic harmony of all seven colors moving together. It is a symbol of God's provision:

> Every good gift and every perfect gift is from above, and comes down from the Father of lights, with whom there is no variableness, neither shadow or turning.[5]

ONEness contains all things in itself. ONEness signifies unity, the common basis between all things. ONE Power is the creative force that causes all things to come into outer manifestation. Symbols of ONEness include the following: the rod, which brings water and fertility; the pen, which releases Word as the sword of truth; the arrow, which brings power and, as the straight line (which is the shortest distance between two points) penetrates its target with its force; the ray, which is a shaft of light coming from Divine Source and returning into It; the "primitive

---

[5]James 1:17, *The Holy Bible* (Cambridge, England: University Press, 1973).

streak"—the first positive sign of character in the future form contained in the egg. This is the forerunner of the spinal column.

Other symbols of ONEness include the finger that points to what is significant; the phallus that impregnates; the flaming torch that kindles others with its light; the fan, a symbol of energies that are contained and unified before spreading out; the "staff of life," which brings supply, nourishment, and abundance; and the magic wand. In psychological thinking, ONE represents the individual ego—a human composite of strength, self-expression in thinking, the bringer of new concepts, initiative, organizer of experience, courage and rulership over the personality.

ONEness contains unity at the center. Akhenaton is reputed to have said that a ruler is ONE nation. A good friend is ONE whom we can trust. In this way a true friend is a person whose diverse aspects are integrated and expressed in such a way that we sense the solidity and unity in the midst of differences.

The Expression of ONEness in the Human Temperament

The path of ONEness energizes the mind. Energy focuses in the thinking; thoughts are quickened by a steady stream of new ideas and dynamic concepts. The movement is usually from abstract to concrete. The presence of Providence offers new opportunities for pioneering and catalytic thinking. Great expectations bring a desire for action, outer form, and expression. The response of ONEness seeks growth and change more than comfort. People activated by the energy of ONEness become trailblazers. The mind spurs them on, buzzing like beehives, filled with a sense of possibilities and good fortune.

If we tap into the power of ONEness, we live a life that is dynamic, a life that surges forward with urgency and immediacy. Mental intensity and life style are highly charged. The path of ONEness calls for risks and the dangers of a pathfinder. It is a path where we rarely know what lies ahead. In the process of creative thinking, the idea in concept often becomes more attractive than the slower, more gradual working out of the idea.

Attitudes and Behaviors of ONEness

People strongly connected to the pathway of ONEness need large measures of autonomy. There must be plenty of room, especially for free thinking, in both jobs and relationships. Such people often resent taking orders or direction; they prefer to be in control themselves, able to think daringly and take initiative whenever they desire to do so. The attitude of ONEness is assertive.

People are not abstractions. It is helpful for those strongly connected to the path of ONEness to see individuals as flesh and blood, not just embodiments of their idea. I remember an acquaintance of mine saying once, "I need people so that I can test my ideas." He, himself, was later tested greatly when he had children, for they expressed feelings and emotions and demanded personal involvement from him.

To express the energy of ONEness, a person will often "implode," concentrating a strong mental focus, like a flame of fire, on a particular interest or idea until it runs dry or until such an individual becomes bored. Then, suddenly, the energy shifts elsewhere. Rapid changes occur continuously in these peoples' lives, and sometimes it is difficult to see the connection from one interest to the next. The energy of ONEness emanates a dedication in the moment, but often people on the path of ONEness have difficulty sustaining interest in a given area for long periods of time. The intensity of the energy of ONEness

requires continuous mental stimulus and new, challenging directions for thought.

Those who demonstrate the way of ONEness often
take the lead; they live on the cutting edge, in the van-
guard. They usually can be seen constantly reading new
articles, listening to new motivational tapes, or attending
"growth" seminars. They are frequently entrepreneurs –
opportunists of the first order. They are very verbal and
need others to talk to (not listen to), bouncing ideas freely
about their environment. Breaking the barriers of old
behaviors and thinking patterns can mean that these individuals are very outspoken, outrageous in their directness
and immediately resourceful. These people do not ever
enjoy repeating.

Interestingly, with the energy of ONEness, often come
the ingredients of Providence and good fortune. Unexpected doors open or a benefactor appears at the crucial
time, or there may be a sudden break that occurs, such as
an inheritance, a windfall, or a patron. New avenues of
opportunity are frequent.

Strengths from the Energy of ONEness

By attuning ourselves to the energy stream of ONEness,
we can develop the power of creative thinking: it is helpful
in a "clear field" area of our lives to be able to think, feel,
and visualize a possibility ahead – to KNOW before actually seeing the physical manifestation of our wishes. The
power of ONEness keeps the mind alert, creative and
single-focused. It is forceful, direct and inspires confidence and a willingness to risk the unknown. In the inspiration of ONEness, we can observe greater assertiveness,
charisma, and leadership; it is magnetic and motivational.
Such energy is always expectant; it is self-starting, not
waiting for others' approval or support. "NOW is the
appointed time."

Values and Creativity of ONEness

In its most constructive expression, the energy stream of ONEness stimulates certain values and quickens consciousness in the following areas:

1) Zeal—the capacity to sustain an eager, active interest in life.

2) Courage—the ability to fight for the good in the midst of danger and adversity.

3) Willpower—strength of intentionality and determination.

4) Initiative—stepping forward with confidence; taking the first step without waiting for proof of success.

The energies of ONEness stimulate definite interest in fields of business and communication. Those stirred by these energies of ONEness often make good problem solvers and trouble-shooters; they can get the job done quickly. They do well in brainstorming and think-tank activities. They affirm the MEGA-vision: nothing need be impossible if they believe strongly enough in it. Such individuals prefer to work their own hours, sometimes intense and irregular, but they give more in a concentrated period of time. They are usually futuristic, not really interested in "reinventing the wheel." They also prefer to hear "the bottom line," rather than indulging in small talk. Thought produces action and feeling.

Observing the Spectrum of ONEness Energy

As people express the energies of the various nine pathways, it is easy to observe a continuum of outer behaviors.

These responses range from underdeveloped to balanced and, finally, from balanced to excessive. Often, in childhood, these varied streams of energy may not have been encouraged sufficiently. Or, there may have been dominant and suppressive conditioning, which can result in either the insufficient expression of the energy or too much of it coming forth, as a form of revolt.

The energy of ONEness in childhood has to do with autonomy and initiative. It can first be seen in early developmental stages, especially during the "toddler" and "preschool" years, so clearly described by John Bradshaw in his book, *Homecoming*, and a host of other writers in the field of child development. In these early years, after the infant stage, each child tends to become more assertive, trying to explore the world and bursting forth on the human scene. Each child has these natural feelings, impulses, and desires, and needs a friendly environment in which to express his or her potentials. The energy of ONEness encourages asking questions and thinking for oneself, as well as stimulating the willingness to risk and take chances, in order to learn. If this dimension in a person is stunted early, it often may take years before a new, healthy assertiveness appears.

People who demonstrate the energy of ONEness show an early predisposition for rapid mental progress, and they tend to obey strongly their own inner timetable of interests and growth. They cannot be easily forced into any predetermined molds of thinking or behavior. They tend to stand alone in their own world of creative thought processes.

The following pages describe the continuum of the energy field of ONEness.

The Underdeveloped Expression of ONEness (–1)

Impetus is lacking.
There may be mental resistance to new ideas.

A person may vacillate in thinking.
Risks are to be avoided.
An individual may wait too long and miss the
     opportunity.
Others are always expected to lead and go first.
The person is not a self-starter.
There is a tendency to remain idle and stuck.
The mind is dormant most of the time.
The person prefers to remain mentally unchallenged.
Behavior is too tentative.
Mental inertia is evident.
It is necessary to be more assertive.

The Balanced Expression of ONEness (1)

The energy is highly stimulating, mentally and verbally.
Life is often bountiful; Providence opens doors.
There is a strong desire for self-actualization.
Pioneer thinking brings new possibilities into being.
Many awakenings and new beginnings occur.
The person takes the initiative with confidence.
Always move forward! Never accept defeat!
Be future-oriented; live on the cutting edge.
Live like a pathfinder, with conviction.
ONEness ignites others and catalyzes others' minds.
Welcome the innovative approach. Be a self-starter!
Let the new vision open now.
Be bold and enterprising. Become an entrepreneur!
Magnetize and manifest what you visualize – without
     harming others.
Cast your bread upon the waters.
Take care of "No. 1" first.
Look to new horizons; live for the untried and
     impossible.
Be ready to risk.
Be independent and work toward autonomy.

Conceive and achieve with zeal.

Accept the challenge.

Be assertive and seize the opportunity.

Use verbal skills and take mental leaps.

Let unity diversify outward.

Live with the incentive to be daring and determined.

The Excessive Expression of ONEness (+ 1)

The individual is filled with self-will and egotism.

Too much ONEness is oblivious to others' feelings and
    needs.

"Know-it-all" behavior predominates.

Mental aggression ridicules and demeans.

Others' ideas are discredited and are treated
    disrespectfully.

Arrogance is customary. The person expects special
    privileges.

There is low tolerance for slower minds.

Megalomania often can be observed.

Ideas are grandiose.

"What I think is good for everyone."

Ideas often prove unworkable.

The individual resents authority and does not take
    orders well.

The individual refuses direction and is not teachable.

Behavior can be impulsive and argumentative.

"It has to be my idea."

Verbally abusive responses agitate and antagonize others.

The crusader must change and convert everyone to a
    certain viewpoint.

The energy is exclusive: there is no interest in what I am
    not a part of.

The vision is too narrow and intense. Power is dry and
    restricted.

"Out of sight, out of mind."

Opportunists go too far and use others to get ahead.

Self-centered, petulant responses always fight the
   system.
Braggadocio combines with obstinate and headstrong
   behaviors.
It is enjoyable to "bait" others.
Better to live in mental euphoria, unable to achieve
   intimacy.
Being a poor listener, the individual may act compul-
   sively, before considering the consequences.
Thinking is powerful but too restricted.
Frozen feelings minimize others' feelings.

Case Studies in the Energy of ONEness

I can think of many people through the years who demonstrate a strong connectedness to the energy stream of
ONEness. "A" was a dynamic, strikingly beautiful
woman, who radiated charisma and authority. She was a
"man's man," who related best with people who were
quick and readily adaptable to her ideas. True to the
energy of ONEness, "A" kept her office moving: new
ideas permeated the atmosphere in such a way that
nobody could really settle in. "A" also rotated the various
responsibilities in her business, so that employees always
were learning new aspects of the trade. "A's" idea was that
everyone could instantly take over for anyone else, should
the need arise. "A" herself trained others to take her own
job, if ever she decided to leave. Likewise, she took many
ongoing workshops and new classes, in order to keep current and maintain contact with all the newest trends. With
buyers, "A" was direct, honest, and to the point.
   At home, "A's" relationships were always exciting:
she remodeled her house regularly and changed the paintings on the walls frequently. She passed quickly through a
"French Impressionist" stage and move into Native American art after a summer trip to Santa Fe, New Mexico. Her
tastes in art were reflected in clothing styles, and when I

last saw her, she served me tea in her Navajo medicine blanket, which she wrapped around her wherever she went. "A's" husband, a more laconic type, never tried to keep up with his wife. Instead he quietly observed "A's" different "stages of growth" and followed his own interests in collecting ancient artifacts. "A" was demanding but fair and unpossessive. She simply asked for room to follow her own leadings and her continuous new interests.

"S" demonstrates the excessive use of ONEness energy. He is in his middle years and behaves intensely and argues frequently. His wife, much younger than "S," must find ways to get her husband's attention. "S" does not encourage his wife to think for herself at all, and frequently undermines, criticizes, and talks down to her. "S" wants to be a writer but at present makes his living in an insurance company. At work he is alert, resourceful, and polite. When he comes home, he criticizes others at work and thinks his superiors are slow. At parties "S" brags about how much he knows. Most of all "S" demonstrates frozen feelings. Because of deep hurts and shaming from his parents, "S" finds it difficult to share feelings with anyone. He always leads with his mind and follows with projects and activities. When his little daughter says, "Daddy, I am feeling sad," he says to her, "Knock it off; I don't want to hear it!" "S" is extremely self-centered. It is very rare that he thinks or talks of others, except if they can serve his own self-seeking ambition. He typifies this description of an egomaniacal person:

> Because self-centered persons place themselves at the center of the universe, everything else is defined by and through them.[6]

---

[6]A. W. Schaef, Co-Dependence (New York: Perennial Library, 1986), pp. 59–60.

In the excessively ONE pattern, it is customary to encounter a "one-track mind," fixated opinions which "should be embraced" by others, a foolish insistence, and an inability to heed advice. Many of these imbalances can best be harmonized by the next energy stream, the pathway of TWOness.

Expanding the Energy of ONEness

1) Develop a plan for improving your verbal skills. Join a group such as Toastmasters, where you have to speak on some topic in front of others. Find ways to express yourself more with words; interact with others through the sharing of ideas.

2) Decide to accept one new leadership position this year. Try to stay with it for at least six months. Notice the ways in which you are assertive with those around you. For your own practice, become involved with one of the following areas: heading up a fund drive, leading a group class or support group, lead an activity in PTA or Scouts, or community projects.

3) Develop a reading program in which you agree to read at least ten new articles a week in new areas of learning. Find the magazines or periodicals in the library. Take notes and talk about them to someone who can understand you.

4) Ask the question, "Whom have I stimulated today with my ideas and conversation?" Avoid meaningless chitchat.

5) Keep a journal and jot down any ideas that come through your mind. Notice how one idea feeds

another. Share your daily journal with a trusted friend.

6) Find a new interest in your life and study this area thoroughly. Make notes on your research.

7) Read a book like *Think and Grow Rich*, by Napoleon Hill, in which you will find important ideas about possibility thinking and creative visualization.

8) Read biographies of famous self-starters, original thinkers and entrepreneurs, such as Benjamin Franklin, Charles Lindburgh, Eleanor Roosevelt, Henry Ford and others.

9) Imagine each day as an occasion for you to receive new seed thoughts from the universe. See the stream of ONEness energy as an abundance of seeds (possibilities) dropping into your receptive consciousness and bearing their fruits as you keep them fresh and watered.

10) Can you find an area of your life that needs more initiative on your part? Do you feel any area in you that is too passive? Find a way to activate your consciousness by taking appropriate boldness and expressing genuine conviction.

The Energy of TWOness

What is most important . . . is to find some consistency, predictability and reliability. . . . The alternative is a sense of mistrust, the feeling that [the other] is unpredictable and unreliable, and may not be there when needed.

—Erik Erikson

A person cannot be said to succeed in this life who does not satisfy one friend.

—Henry David Thoreau

The most important thing is to do the other one good, because for that purpose alone was man sent into this life.

—Douglas V. Steere

Keys to TWOness

Certain themes emanate from the energy of TWOness. These focus in areas of practicality and sensitivity. Especially important are emotional issues that center around partnership, trust and affiliation. Consider the following questions:

1) Are you inclined to feel lonely and needy when someone you feel especially close to is not near?

2) Are you fully present with another when you are together?

3) Is it difficult for you to trust someone you do not feel personally close to?

4) Do you go out of your way to avoid conflict and confrontations?

5) Do you prefer jobs and a life style that offer security and comfort?

6) Do you enjoy handling details and cleaning up "messes?"

7) Are you more at ease with one friend at a time than with two, three, or a group?

8) Do you often sense another person's need without being told?

9) Is it important to you to feel needed?

10) Do you prefer being supportive more than leading?

These inquiries bring into awareness the common themes of TWOness, especially those concerned with intimacy, one-on-one partnership, safety, sensitivity, and connectedness with people or with data and information.

The Energy of TWOness
in World Symbolism

In the history of world symbolism, the energy of TWO-
ness is significant in many areas. The essence of TWOness
signifies the descent of Spirit into material forms. In the
conjunction of Spirit and matter,[1] TWO moves out of the
unity of ONE in order to become selective in matter. Thus,
TWOness expresses separation and antithesis; TWOness
emphasizes polarity and the duality of manifested life.[2]
TWOness implies imitation, division, comparison, and
contrast with another. TWOness, feeling separated from
the unity of ONEness, tends to be more anxious and need-
fully receptive: it is a mirroring energy that sees and recognizes itself through the other. TWOness recognizes differences, such as the alternating currents of cycles and
seasons. TWOness is sympathetic and identifies with the
experiences and feelings of the other. TWOness learns
from the movement of antagonism, "a contest" and complementary opposition between different forces. In biol-
ogy, TWOness can be observed as a creative interference
between TWO dissimilar energies, such as a seed pushing
against the soil, in order to produce growth and fruition.

The energy of TWOness expresses the double standard: a person lives with one foot on earth and one in the
heavens, thus trying to maintain balance. In this way
TWOness is selective and discriminates, continuously
needing to create new unity out of duality. TWOness is
the harmonious combination of "explicit and implicit."[3]

Duality urges each of us onward to work out increasing balance and progression. TWOness is an energy,
therefore, which stimulates us to reconcile existing differ-

[1]L. D. Balliett, *Vibration of Numbers* (London: L. N. Fowler, 1905), p. 23.
[2]Geoffrey Hodson, *The Hidden Wisdom of the Bible* (Adyar, India: Theosophical
Publishing House, 1963), vol I, p. 146.
[3]G. Hodson, p. 147.

ences, while moving toward the greater Infinite: "Infinite progression, through the pairs of opposites, is the Divine Law of Manifestation in duality."[4] The exact expression of balance is never quite attainable on earth. We find the square root of TWO is incapable of perfect division. Thus, TWOness leads us into Infinity, the only dimension where perfect harmony can be experienced: "Pairs of opposites cannot be (perfectly) balanced on the physical plane without calling into play an Infinite factor—a force from the higher, superphysical realms."[5] TWOness rarely feels secure by itself.

The energy of TWOness stimulates in each of us the sense of "the other," as the one who can provide the best sense of the lost unity of ONE. Thus, TWOness quickens the feelings of measuring life by feeling comparison—in pairs of opposites—yang and yin, male and female, known and mysterious, leading and following, direct and roundabout, acting and waiting, decided and receptive, obvious and subtle, dry and fluidic, objective and subjective, closure and openness, attraction and repulsion, sound and silence, clear and shadow, tension and release, waking and sleeping, etc. The ancient Theosophical Masons, Pythagoreans and others realized how much TWOness energy is connected to finding balance out of the great "contrarieties"—the multitude of polarities and opposites existing in earthly life.[6]

We can observe many objects and symbols that embody the energy of TWOness: the "father" and "mother" aspects of God's Presence have been represented as "a consuming fire" (masculine) and "love" (feminine); the TWO-edged sword brings confrontation and peace; a bridge, the line across the space between TWO

4F. H. & H. Curtiss, *Key to the Universe*, p. 86.
5F. H. & H. Curtiss, *Key to the Universe*, p. 86.
6G. Oliver, *The Pythagorean Theorem* (Minneapolis, MN: Wizard's Book Shelf, 1975), p. 62.

points, connects and harmonizes distance and division; the cross lifts the flatness of earth's hardness into higher, vertical sources of Light; a couple contains complementary energies that can work together for harmonious outcomes; a team of TWO works hand in hand to produce greater power than is possible through singular efforts; the heart consists of TWO chambers that form one unit; the brain is bi-cameral and works best in the balance of alternating currents moving in the left and right hemispheres; the twin, who feels so closely to another; the soulmate—our biune complement and mathematical opposite, and all pairs, who work creatively, TWO by TWO.

In Chinese thought, TWOness represents "goodness and humaneness." The symbol for TWO, "jen," the number, also means "person doubled" or person-to-personness, the realization of the inherent moral nature that is included in the relationship of one person to another.[7]

The energy of TWOness implies sacrifice and unification that is achieved, even after misfortune may have resulted. TWOness means "opinion," the capacity to "see straight ahead and not to think in curves."[8] TWOness is patient and enduring amidst conditions that are temporal, transient and fleeting. It is an emblem of fortitude and courage, yielding the vision of the seer who can see with the heart.

TWOness is the energy of the feminine principle, the "mater" (mother of earth), the prostrate feminine—sleeping, silent, waiting, mysterious, hidden. TWOness is the eventual producer of gender—male/female in life forms. TWOness draws others to itself with the power of its purity.

---

[7]R. Taylor, *They Shall Not Hurt* (Boulder, CO: Colorado Association University Press, 1989), p. 53.
[8]Balliett, p. 23.

The Expression of TWOness in the Human Temperament

As the energy of ONEness stimulates the mind, the power of TWOness awakens supportiveness and the emotional capacity to express partnership. TWOness is an energy that reminds a person of the need to feel secure. Safety is more likely when a person is needed by someone significantly close. TWOness needs a mate—an intimate relationship with another. It's important to affiliate and bond deeply. Most often this is with another person; less often, a close bond may occur with animals or nature. A more cerebral type of person may express TWOness in needing to bond closely with data and information, connecting with facts which replace human and interpersonal contact. This kind of response is more likely in cases where a person's emotions were denied in childhood. Fears of rejection and abandonment can cause "frozen feelings" in adulthood, causing the individual to focus on things or details rather than on unreliable human beings. For a person afraid of losing control, interaction with another person is uncertain and risky. Facts and figures are far more predictable and less resistant to arrangement.

In the energy of TWOness, the desire for concreteness replaces abstract concepts and possibilities for the future. Trust and intimacy are established through close, continuous contact, day by day. Arbitration and selectivity communicate clear desires and choices. Being second and supportive is preferable to taking the lead; remaining in the background is more comfortable than attaining notoriety. The primary comfort zone is established by surrounding oneself with familiar landmarks and a safe environment that allows for the expression of details and personal concerns.

People who tap into the energy stream of TWOness need emotional stability and a low-stress environment.

They do not do as well with sudden changes and pressures. Because they are giving a great deal emotionally, their antennae are always reaching out, and they tend to be overly sensitive and vulnerable. In the energy of TWOness, a close relationship builds on trust and encouragement. A sense of identity emerges from being needed and from doing and existing for someone else. The energy of TWOness makes a person more attentive and agreeable. If people emanating the power of TWOness feel compatible with someone, they will do almost anything for that person; if they do not feel emotionally drawn to someone, they can quickly become very distant.

Those who are strongly oriented toward the energy of TWOness like to keep in touch. They "check in" often, feeling more comfortable if they keep close tabs on someone they care about. They may keep a photo near, a little note or some other momento that reminds them of emotional nearness. They love the little keepsakes and remembrances of life; they gain by seeing the world in conjunction with someone else who becomes the lens for their own significance and meaning.

Attitudes and Behaviors of TWOness

In the energy of TWOness there is a strong personal feeling. People expressing this energy stream may often feel that comments and remarks are being directed just toward themselves, even though others may not have ever had them in mind. The way of TWOness does not handle triangles well. "One at a time" is the motto. These people don't like to give attention to more than one person at a time. More than one person becomes a weakening experience, a threat to intimacy and attention. They consider it best to show complete attention in attending to and listening to "the other" in a relationship. At times, it is better to defer—but not always.

The basic response to TWOness is to emphasize details, neatness, order, and cleanliness. Punctuality means that there is consideration for the other's sensibilities. The focus is more upon pieces than the whole, which often results in losing sight of the overview or the larger perspective. Vignettes, cameos, and miniatures are full of appeal.

The minutiae of life must be balanced and coordinated so that by arranging things well, a secure feeling emerges, and then these people can expand into larger vistas. Loose ends must be tied together well, before there can be freedom of movement: furniture, dishes, or flowers have their appropriate place; a checkbook must be balanced to the penny; silverware and clothes must be arranged and folded neatly in a drawer; and telephone numbers are best kept alphabetically in an address book. Other people are most appealing when they are well-groomed and smell clean. A tidy system thus provides timesaving and emotional security. "The more I feel good about myself, the more I will take care of myself, as well as cleaning up after others."

The energy of TWOness emphasizes the ability to communicate closely through feelings. A simple touch, close rapport, a refined atmosphere, gentleness and appropriateness help to engender intimacy and connectedness. You can sense how others are feeling by the way they look and act. It is essential to be trustworthy: what is shared in confidence must remain in the private vaults of secrecy—to the grave. And in times of trouble, try to be a harmonizer and a peacemaker: conciliate where possible. Be a good listener, a keen observer, and keep clear and receptive to the atmosphere around you. Be caring without becoming possessive or too clinging. Likewise, don't let your kindness be made into a doormat for others' selfishness or inconsiderate behavior. Remember your limits! Be practical and intimate, but not weak or dependent.

Know when to speak and when to remain quiet; wait for the best timing and be careful about how much you reveal yourself. Give but don't give yourself away.

Strengths from the Energy of TWOness

In summary the main strengths of the power of TWOness are as follows: there is an ability to show emotional closeness, loyalty and intimate partnership; stability emerges from sharing special times together; taking pains and being attentive yields the most desirable outcome; being a good listener insures close connection; knowing how to blend and accompany well avoids conflicts; by giving much to another, it is also important to receive that person's participation, not just support from the side; learn how to be considerate and cooperative, moderate, selective and cautious; try to relieve anxiety by getting the facts, information and background; be aware of the intricacies and details of a situation; be precise and painstaking, especially when emotionally involved; remain receptive at all times.

Values and Creativity of TWOness

The power stream of TWOness emphasizes the following values:

1) Humility—the absence of pride or arrogance; ability to show modesty and courtesy; capacity to live "low to the earth."

2) Self-Control—able to be in charge of one's emotional and behavioral responses.

3) Patience—waiting and enduring, while working for something better.

4) Teachableness—meekness; the willingness to learn without resistance or delay.

5) Punctuality—being on time for appointments and meeting promptly whatever is due.

6) Discernment—accuracy in evaluating better versus worse.

7) Refinement—demonstrating appropriate response in each situation and relationship.

8) Peacemaker—"Blessed are the peacemakers, for they shall be called the children of God." (Matthew 5:9)

9) Holy Obedience—being ready and surrendered to doing what life asks and requires; not fighting circumstances or the process.

10) Sincerity—being truly who you are, without pretense.

In work and creative self-expression, those who demonstrate the energy of TWOness appreciate order, sensitivity and accuracy. They need an environment that is secure and relatively free from stress. They are especially good in "getting pieces together," and they are often quite skilled at straightening out the unfinished projects and "messes" of others. These people, who are strongly attuned to the energies of TWOness, will eventually resent working where they are not really needed or valued. Rarely are they in the positions of leadership, yet those who are in charge will often seek out such a person for counsel and advice. The energies of TWOness are more often introverted and move from feelings to action and thought.

Observing the Spectrum of TWOness Energy

The basic themes of TWOness center around issues of trust and emotional closeness. The pathway of energy, identified as TWOness, is stimulated in each of us immediately when we are born. In the beginning stage of life, infancy, the baby is totally dependent upon a stable caretaker. As infants we want to feel as soon as possible that someone comforting is going to be there for us, attending to our needs. Close bonding with someone who is safe and offers the ingredient of security is essential for the baby. If this basic feeling of stability and emotional closeness is not satisfied, and if the predisposition toward this need is especially strong in certain people, feelings of anxiety, worry and insecurity may be present for them much of the lifetime. Such people may spend a large part of their life looking for someone to be there for them, emotionally, continuously reassuring them, "needing" them, and taking care of them. In order to feel safe and needed, not abandoned, such people in childhood may play out unhealthy roles, such as being the victim, the slave, the helpless baby, the scapegoat, or the hypochondriac, who receives extra attention from others even if it is punishment.

As the basic emotional needs of trust, intimacy, and bondedness are met, people who are strongly connected to the pathway of TWOness gain confidence. They express a balanced contact with this energy by becoming good affiliators, harmonizers, and receptive, intuitive sensors to others. They can then be considerate, supportive interpreters of others' needs, without absorbing them into themselves. Excessive release of this energy results in hypercritical behaviors and the tendency to be obsessive about details.

The Underdeveloped Expression of TWOness (–2)

There is a deep underlying fear of abandonment.
The person lacks a sense of validity and always needs to be needed.
There is too much hesitancy and timidity.
Anxiety comes from feeling cut off from unity.
Fear of rejection produces feelings of isolation and loneliness.
Wimpy behavior prevents direct action (mousy attitude).
The person is too submissive, lacks a fighting spirit, and, too easily acquiescing, will put up with anything.
Pouting is frequent and this individual looks for attention.
Masochistic tendencies permit others to be abusive and intrusive.
The person frequently gets sick and often becomes a hypochondriac.
It is easy to feel guilty and inferior: poor me!
A sense of helplessness makes the person become a victim.
Reassurance from anyone is desired; self-pity seeks sympathy.
Beating around the bush makes the person seem devious and sneaky.
A worrywart approach to life becomes habitual.
The game of "keeping others guessing" is appealing and gets attention.
The person looks too much to others for a sense of happiness.
The world becomes too tiny, sheltered, and claustrophobic.
Others feel stifled because of too much clinging.
The person stays glued to the "vacant hope."
Too much fretfulness leads to phobias and panic attacks.

A sponge-like lack of boundaries causes one to absorb
   others totally.
Too much vulnerability leaves the doors wide open for
   invasion.
Taking things too personally, an individual becomes para-
   noid and always feels persecuted.
Overly sentimental responses lead to hysteria.
The person is a whiner, who always wants to be babied.
Wet blankets always doubt the good.
The person who is too passive always takes the blame.
Troubled feelings often need pacifying.
The person needs pampering and continuous TLC.

The Balanced Expression of TWOness (2)

TWOness gains through association, affiliation, and
   supportiveness.
It is healthy to accept our vulnerability and limitations.
The person wants participation, not just support. Be a
   partner!
Personal sharing of feelings and closeness is most
   desired.
Humility and patience open doors. Harmony reigns.
Pay attention to the little things, emphasize details, and
   enjoy life's cameos.
Feedback is expected frequently as well as the opportunity
   "to process" feelings.
Peacemakers and harmonizers are good listeners.
Get the facts, data, and statistics.
Attend immediately to what is at hand.
Appreciate refinement! Observe proportion and appropri-
   ate measure!
Be gentle and teachable!
Avoid stress and complications.
Sudden changes are difficult to handle emotionally.

Security and comfort are essential. Communicate your
     needs.
Sympathetic response brings closeness. Diplomacy is
     useful.
It is wise to play safe and to be cautious and careful.
A considerate person shares with others in ways that are
     comforting.
The person is tidy and punctual.
Cooperation may sometimes mean accommodation.
The person thrives on encouragement, validation, special
     handling, and personal affection.
Often a selective attitude makes life more exclusive.
Intimacy means personalizing and particularizing.
Take time for minutiae.
Mirror others' moods without absorbing them.
It feels better to support than to lead.
Build bridges, not chasms.
TWOness is receptive artistically.
Often the need is to straighten out other people's messes.
"TWO is the power behind the throne, unheralded and
     unseen, yet innermost the heart and life of all created
     essences."[9]

The Excessive Expression of TWOness (+2)

The person hovers over others, not giving them sufficient
     space.
There is a feeling of "uptightness" and being edgy.
The person frequently finds fault and is never content.
Being retaliatory and vindictive becomes a habit.
It is easy to nit-pick persons and situations "to death."
Being possessive of others is customary.
It's always easy to see what's wrong.

---

[9]C. Heline, p. 9.

Chattering on about trivia and "motor-mouthing" hide
    anxiety.
For attention, create a crisis.
Obsessive and compulsive behaviors predominate.
The alarmist always is the bearer of bad tidings.
Complicate everything to keep things focused on you.
Offer incessant reminders to get attention.
Pick everything apart.
The person can be a tattler, always agitating about life.
Making a mountain out of a molehill, the individual seems
    to be a real fussbudget.
It is easy to get buried in details.
Hypervigilance becomes "hawkishness."
The person is always on guard; never relaxed.
An extremely critical nature can be cruelly blunt.

Case Study in the Energies of TWOness

The journey into harmony and balance is challenging for
people strongly connected to the energy stream of TWO-
ness. Because there may be feelings of isolation and fear of
rejection and abandonment, these people may begin by
demonstrating some of the characteristics of underdeveloped TWOness (-2): Miss T., a young woman I remember
very clearly, began by being so needy and desperate for
company that she accepted any relationship, even one
which was hurtful to her. She talked to me about her
younger days when she was co-dependent on any person
that even showed any signs of liking her. She felt that she
did not have any genuine sense of meaning in her own
right and therefore all significance and self-worth came
from outside herself, from others who paid attention to
her. She noticed that when she felt unneeded, she became
worried and "more negative." She then began to cling,
even more tightly, to whatever person was in her life, and
found that this behavior alienated her from others. When

a relationship failed, Miss T. went into her "marshmallow" role, becoming overly apologetic, submissive and, later, resentful. She would even play sick to try to get some attention from somewhere.

Miss T.'s life changed radically when she was hired at a neighborhood school. Many of the children she met were very needy, and some came from backgrounds of neglect and abuse. Slowly, Miss T. realized there were others far needier. She became an advocate and protector of the children; in this way her confidence increased. Somebody really needed her daily. Miss T.'s melancholia and sad-faced appearance dropped away because her new sense of significance was not based on weakness.

As time went on, Miss T. became more confident in her own right. Criticism from others no longer wounded her as deeply, because she had too many responsibilities that took her time and attention. She also felt the children's trust, and her supervisor looked to her frequently and valued her expertise. Miss T. no longer needed to be a victim, scapegoat, or a helpless "marshmallow." She had a cause and work to look forward to, and new relationships developed out of her work and a growing sense of worth.

Expanding the Energy of TWOness

1) At regular intervals throughout the day, practice remembering a loved one. Try to sense, feel, and imagine where that person may be during different moments. What is he or she doing, saying, feeling, etc.? (A good exercise for building intimacy.)

2) Fill up a page in your journal with suggestions for being more considerate toward another person that you know, including yourself.

3) If you happen to be more self-sufficient, choose one area of your life and ask for help with it from someone else. Choose to let a loved one "in" to help you in an area that you would be more likely to handle yourself. Be a good receiver.

4) At least once a week, for 15 minutes, try to perform a detailed task. Pull weeds, water the garden, clean some rooms, wash the clothes, etc.

5) Take over a task involving small details for a stated amount of time. Do this for someone you love.

6) Devote at least 10 minutes a day to being a better listener. Show deeper interest in others' concerns and comments.

The
Energy
of
THREEness

Wonder excites activity. When wonder is recovered in scattered places, the lighting of its fires here and there and the power of its silences will set up a chain of cryptic rumors, like the spreading announcement of liberation in a captive land.

—Alan Tory

I think of the earth as the floor of a great cathedral where altar and Presence are everywhere. . . . I realize the golden world is all about me in imperishable beauty . . ., and I know an eternal love is within me and around me, pressing upon me and sustaining with infinite tenderness my body, soul and spirit.

—AE

Keys to THREEness

The energy of THREEness has its own specific thematic content, which centers around creativity and self-expression. To see how strongly connected you are to this stream of power, consider these questions:

1) Is it important for you to express beauty and joy through the creative arts, such as painting, reading or writing poetry, performing or listening to music, etc.?

2) Is it easy for you to live in your dreams and feelings, especially in the world of memories?

3) Do you often feel like a romantic, in love with life?

4) Is it important for you to bring beauty into your atmosphere—into your home, office, restaurants, etc.?

5) Are you selective about the colors you wear each day?

6) Are you easily able to visualize places and conditions that appeal to you?

7) When going to the movies, is it easy for you to lose yourself in the world of feelings expressed by the actors and actresses?

8) In talking to others, do you find yourself becoming very dramatic, often talking with gestures and emotion?

9) When out driving or going to work, are you usually "somewhere else" during the trip?

10) Do you live more in the drama of the moment—in spontaneity, rather than in the structure of plans, goals and schedules?

The inventory of questions will center you in the major themes of THREEness: imagination, joy and creativity.

The Energy of THREEness in World Symbolism

In the symbolism of numbers, THREEness offers many fascinating insights. The receptivity of TWO leads into the expression of beauty—THREE. THREEness thus restores feelings and emotions to a new equilibrium that involves personal, creative self-expression and imagination. THREEness is an energy that brings synthesis of conception (ONE) and selectivity (TWO). The living are "THREE times blessed," able to manifest creation in the expression of "time, space and form."[1]

The energy of THREEness connects a person to the knowledge and vibrations of the Heavenly Bodies, often manifesting as a mysterious and spatial quality that seems to keep the creative individual somewhat elusive—here and not here. THREEness is the essence of the arts and creativity; THREE, in the mind of the ancient Greeks, referred to the Mistress of Music. Thus, the energy of THREEness helps a person to describe artistically one's relationship with heaven, earth and all human beings:

> Numbers such as *three*, emblem of heaven,
> earth and man, along with its multiples
> and combinations, reflect the relationships
> which the Chinese believe animate the
> universe.[2]

Through imagination and creative self-expression, a person finds in the energies of THREEness unlimited ways to describe a connection in life with beauty, joy, and drama. THREEness connects us to the magical lands, far away

---

[1]E. Wilson, *You and the Universe* (San Diego, CA: Harmonial Publishers, 1925), p. 53.
[2]A. Juliano, *Treasures of China* (London, England: Penguin Books, 1981), p. 46.

and out of time—the realms of our hearts' desires and our dreams.

THREEness describes three basic ways in which people direct their energies: *cardinal*, moving ahead like an arrow; *fixed*, focusing and concentrating deeply; and *mutable*, diversifying in many directions at once. In the zodiac there are three groups of signs that describe these three types of movement: Aries (cardinal fire), Cancer (cardinal water), Libra (cardinal air), and Capricorn (cardinal earth); Taurus (fixed earth), Leo (fixed fire), Scorpio (fixed water), and Aquarius (fixed air); Gemini (mutable air), Virgo (mutable earth), Sagittarius (mutable fire), and Pisces (mutable water).

The energy of THREEness is like a tripod, providing a stable, circular base and focusing energy upward, like a cone, to emerge in a single point of focus. This point of fusion exposes the resolution of opposites into a new creative harmony.

THREEness is expressed in the three-syllabled, holy word, A-U M, meaning peace. Alertness, in the midst of peacefulness, is tolled by the sounds of the Angelus Bell, rung THREE times a day, with a peal of 3 times 3, signifying the 9 heavenly hierarchies of angels: Seraphim, Cherubim, Thrones, Dominions, Virtues, Powers, Principalities, Archangels and Angels.

Various trinities and groups of THREE emerge in world symbolism: the Holy Trinity: Father, Son, and Holy Spirit; Brahma (Creator aspect of God), Vishnu (Preserver and stabilizing aspect of God), and Shiva (Destroyer and changing, transformational aspect of God); God (Theos), Word (Logos), and Soul (Psyche), attributed by Plato; the THREEness of body, soul, and spirit; THREE primary colors: red, yellow, and blue; THREE processes of unfoldment: purification, illumination, and initiation; THREE qualities of space: finite, indefinite, and infinite; THREE determinates of form: length, breadth, and thickness;

THREE stages/cycles of growth: thesis, antithesis, and synthesis; the THREEness of father, mother, and child, and the Fates, Furies, and Graces of ancient mythology. THREE Wise Men, Gaspar, Melchior, and Balthasar, are traditionally mentioned in the New Testament account of the birth of Christ Jesus. Finally, the emblem of the Irish nation is the shamrock, a three-lobed leaf. These and many other examples describe the essence of THREEness in world symbolism.

The Expression of THREEness in the Human Temperament

Like the energy stream of TWOness, the power of THREE-ness also focuses itself through the human feelings and emotions. However, the actual themes differ widely. In the stream of THREEness, what is most important is the creativity, inspiration, and beauty. The energy of THREE-ness describes potentials and responses that are open and flowing, joyous, expansive, and spatial. Ambience and nuance are beautiful for their own sake, without any specific intentionality. The way of THREEness quite simply enjoys: it contains fewer lines and more curves; less measuredness and more flare.

Attitudes and Behaviors of THREEness

People who express a strong sense of THREEness are often emotional romantics. They may prefer to live in their dreams more than in the actual, "real" world. For them the imagination is more captivating than what is concrete, tangible, and mundane. They prefer to flow in the stream of consciousness, living in the present moment of delight, filled with the spontaneity of feeling, taking it as it comes without much planning ahead, and always remaining in love with life.

The energy of THREEness affirms beauty for its own sake. Often, the particular characteristics of the Beautiful are hidden in the larger atmosphere of ugliness and insensitivity. Thus beauty is much like the diamond in the rough, a rare treasure temporarily covered over with dirt, or like an enchantment previously obscured. Therefore, what stimulates the person connected to THREEness is the quality of beauty that opens each of us to the sense of wonder and awe. Beauty frees us to feel the magnificent splendor—the underlying goodness that surrounds us like a free gift from the heart of the Infinite. In the midst of beauty, we realize the amazing abundance that fills our lives:

> Every good desire [and dream]
> of the heart shall be fulfilled,
> either in ways that we anticipate,
> or in ways that in God's sight
> are even better.[3]

The essence of THREEness is often elusive. The Muse of creativity and inspiration cannot be pinned down or captured. The energy of THREEness lives on the wings of fancy, always just out of reach. At times, people who strongly express THREEness may seem like unreachable balloons, floating and drifting in their own spheres of color, only to vanish across the distant horizon. Likewise, these people may seem like mere floaters through life, following their dreams to find new fascination and magic. Such individuals remain winsome, often childlike and beyond one's grasp. They manage to keep others in pursuit but, in the end, leave only a teasing glimpse, a caprice or pleasing wisp—an arabesque that curls its sarabande beyond a distant caravan, vanishing in the shifting sands to Samarkand—enchantment, forever.

---

[3]E. Wilson, *Every Good Desire* (New York: Harper & Row, 1973), p. 5.

Strengths from the Energy of THREEness

We can describe the outstanding strengths of the energy of THREEness as follows: the power of THREEness brings joy, beauty, and upliftment into the atmosphere, chiefly through the arts and creative self-expression; celebration and festivity are quickened; a greater imagination is able to notice what is unusual, mysterious, incredible, and even bizarre; THREEness makes the "impossible dream" more visible; it is an energy that can bring good cheer, good fortune, and a more happy-go-lucky approach to stress; it opens our "inner room" of color and intuition; it opens cloudbursts of vision for the future, often accompanied by invention and praise; THREEness fills our lives with adornment, beautification, decoration, and costume; THREEness makes merry, awakens a new enthusiasm, a "carnival spirit," and releases the gift of laughter. Life is a continuous celebration.

Values and Creativity of THREEness

The energy of THREEness highlights the following values:

1) Holy Expectancy – the continuous ability to live as though the Good that is coming is just around the corner; always looking for the Good.

2) Radiant Joy – the capacity to rejoice and be glad.

3) Inspiration – openness to the inpouring Spirit of life.

4) Wonder – being able to experience the "ah" of creation.

5) Imagination—the power to picture and feel something before it may actually become manifest in the world.

6) Creativity—the ability to fashion something from nothing; realizing more than just what seems to be present.

7) Celebration—to proclaim outwardly and call to remembrance that which quickens our sensitivity.

In the wonderful creativity of THREEness energy, there is room for originality and the self-expression of talents. The pristine "isness" of life emerges in the ocean wave, the white sail in an orange sunset, the glow of beauty smiling, a sinuous form in movement, dancing the dance of life, a rainy night, a tropical garden, mists that cover a mountain peak, a cloudburst in the dry desert, a lone flower on the prairie, etc. In countless sights, sounds, fragrances, and tastes, art becomes the visibility of feelings. THREEness is the cinema of feeling.

The energy of THREEness means being alive to life's continuous changes and metamorphoses: everything is always becoming something else as the seasons of life pass by. Li Po, the ancient Chinese sage and poet, captures these feelings in the following lines:

Why do I live among the green mountains?
I laugh and answer not; my soul is serene:
It dwells in another heaven and earth
belonging to no man.
The peach trees are in flower,
and the water flows on.[4]

4Li Po, quoted in R. H. Blyth, *Zen in English Literature and Oriental Classics* (New York: E. P. Dutton, 1960), p. 46.

As the writer Geoffrey Hodson and others point out, in the spirit of THREEness, the great angels of form and music continue to inspire composers, painters, writers, dancers, and all artists who are receptive to higher imagination. In similar ways the angels, devas, and invisible helpers quicken the powers of nature and our awareness of the wonder and beauty that come through the higher dimensions of consciousness. The energy of THREEness animates the feelings and heightens our perceptive awareness. Feelings move into appropriate expressive activity.

Observing the Spectrum of THREEness Energy

In childhood the energy of THREEness comes through the dimensions of fantasy, storytelling, dramatics, the arts, and one's own dreamworld. A person who shows a clear predisposition for the pathway of THREEness often demonstrates early ability in the arts and may live in a different world: the world of imagination. In schools there needs to be a place for dreamers. Parents may learn much wisdom from a "seemingly" crazy or "far out" story or scene that a child describes. In this area of creativity, what often seems "spaced out" may prove to be a sensitive, accurate, and beautiful attunement to presences and worlds beyond the outer senses.

Isn't it amazing how much we feel and receive indirectly—in ways that are not always apparent, logical, or structured! The pathway of THREEness opens the doors to worlds of beauty, joy, celebration, and praise. In its balanced expression, new horizons and colors open; a song comes through, and there is always room to enter a new ambience and find a way to visit some mysterious place: a place in one's garden of imaginative delights.

Excessive expression of THREEness means too much imagination at the expense of groundedness. Instead of maintaining a joyful connection with their "inner child," such people might become childish, not childlike. Excessive THREEness also means people who never grow up or never seem to interpret daily life accurately. They may remain the eternal "little boy," who looks outside for the fairy princess instead of integrating that side of his feminine self within. In a different way, others might be lifelong "little girls," expecting the knight on the white steed to appear in shining armor, with no shadows, to carry them away to live happily ever after—in luxury.

The Underdeveloped Expression of THREEness (–3)

The capacity to feel the beautiful is not sufficiently present.
Efforts are imitative more than personally creative.
There are feelings of being locked up inside oneself.
Creative hobbies are noticeably absent.
Enjoyment is rarely expressed.
Romantic moments in relationships are few.
There is little sense of soaring or "taking wing."
Self-deprecating attitudes may be present.
Responses are neither joyful nor spontaneously happy.
The person is too particular to be able to "flow along."
The sense of wonder is not visible.
Color, music, drama, and poetry are not seen as interesting.
The person finds it difficult to visualize a desire or dream.
Life is caught in drabness.
Romantic gestures or comments cause embarrassment.
The person prefers to slog along rather than dance to life.
The person rarely seems "turned on" by life.

The Balanced Expression of THREEness (3)

Life is sweet ecstasy, and many moments are filled with
joy and wonder.

Responses are expressed with originality and feeling.

Expectancy fills the air. Enthusiasm is everywhere.

Sudden inspiration is preferable to planning and
structure.

A sense of abundance and plenty relieves difficult
conditions.

Each moment becomes a performance.

A spatial approach to each day tries to keep life open and
promising.

Life is a celebration: sing your song and wear your colors.

Conversation proceeds more by free association and
gladness.

Results come from a "stream of consciousness" approach.

The traveler is happy-go-lucky. Live the dance!

It is easier to live in one's dreams.

"Let's pretend!"

Feel the drama and enjoy an audience.

Remember to "taste the honey" and "smell the roses."

Effusive and bubbly feelings keep the glow alive.

Experience the fragrance of life's charms and
enchantment.

Move in the flavor of ambience and nuance.

The person becomes a winsome weaver of possibilities.

Merriment, good cheer, mirth and jollity abound.

There is nothing like a magical story.

Fairy tales can come true.

The person takes delight in personal self-expression.

The child is alive—beautiful in the land of make-believe.

Hear the music!

The Excessive Expression of THREEness (+3)

Non sequiturs are frequent in conversations.
The person is too flighty, even fickle.
The dream becomes quixotic and too "spaced out."
Euphoria becomes an easy escape from reality.
Histrionic, theatrical responses are frequent.
"Flaky" and escapist behaviors try to avoid responsibility.
It is easier to live in one's fantasies, remaining elusive and
    whimsical.
The truth becomes greatly embellished.
Selective inattention replaces focus and accountability.
The person prefers luxury and is easily flattered and
    charmed.
The inner child becomes infantile and childish.
A dilettante approach lacks depth.
Behaviors can easily become frivolous.
Scruples are lax or nonexistent.
The beautiful dreamer dreams on.
The attitude of the prima donna always seeks the
    spotlight.
Infatuation and "being in love with love" make long-term
    relationships impossible.
Responses are often grandiose.
Life becomes a prelude to living.
Living in illusions, the person is likely to believe anyone
    who believes and feeds them.
It is easier to look for the "joy ride" and the knight in
    shining armor.
Responses are like a butterfly, flitting from flower to
    flower.
A lack of clarity keeps life ephemeral and vague.
Sitting in a chair, the person seems absent in the flesh.
The person's appearance is like the dandy or the
    coquette.

The person is gullible and overly susceptible to others' charms.

By identifying too deeply with others' feelings, the person merges so completely that the individual loses his or her own identity and fails to maintain boundaries or limits.

Injury may come from dissociation and losing oneself too far into a world of sensation and feeling.

Case Study in the Energies of THREEness

One of the most remarkable women I have known is today a very talented violinist in a major symphony orchestra. She did not always have time to pursue her musical career, especially during the earlier years when she raised four children. As time went on, however, in her middle years, she emerged in the true spirit of THREEness. When her marriage ended, she moved to the country, deep in the hills, where she was surrounded by beautiful mountains and the haunting sense of Indians who had lived in the area many years before she arrived. Her love of animals surfaced again, and she took in many strays in the area. She did not have much money, and many times she was near the breaking point, but she hung on and moved forward. Her love of life and music and nature sustained her.

I met her in a creative writing class that I was teaching, and J. showed instant talent, turning out stories that were magical and deeply involving. Her romanticism about being a pioneer woman became reality as she fought ahead, gradually adding on to her modest mobile home and keeping on with her art. Today, she has clearly turned the corner; she is still filled with the same joy and love of life, and she still knows how to laugh and cry at whatever challenges arise. Her lifelong dream of traveling to Europe has just recently come true. She remains in love with life

and her twelve dogs, three horses, goats, sheep, and cats
. . . . The music of life lives in her, and her melody plays
on.

Expanding the Energy of THREEness

1) Take a ride on a merry-go-round; reach for the golden ring.

2) Visit the local zoo and photograph at least three animals.

3) Look into a kaleidoscope for five minutes a day.

4) Listen to a great symphony or concerto. Sing any parts that you like.

5) Walk along the ocean barefoot. Feel the sand sifting between your toes.

6) Listen to the ocean waves at night, either alone or in the arms of a loved one.

7) Watch the sunset for seven evenings in a row. Feel the afterglow!

8) Wear a color you have never worn before.

9) Visit an art gallery and browse through the paintings.

10) Go to a performance of the ballet or folk dancers.

11) Collect seashells with a child; build castles in the sand.

12) Look at the galaxies through a telescope or at a space museum.

13) Go boating or canoeing on a lake. Float without a motor.

14) Photograph the same place or person on ten different occasions.

15) Keep a daily journal for one month, in which you write only about three people or places.

16) Close your eyes during a beautiful piece of music; visualize whatever colors or shapes you might feel through the sounds and melodies.

17) Listen to tapes of great poetry and dramas.

18) Take a pottery class.

19) Take your best friend to a play.

20) Plant your own flowers and imagine how you want to see your garden.

21) Cook a meal for a friend; with the friend's eyes closed, feed him or her the food, piece by piece. Identify the food only by smell.

22) Make every day a celebration; celebrate some thing, person, or event each day in your consciousness.

The Energy of FOURness

The work is our only way of expressing our love for God. Our love must pour on someone . . . . Let us be open to God so that He can use us . . . . We are co-workers of Christ, a *laboring*, fruitbearing branch of the vine.

—*Mother Teresa*

In the praise of God a person is like an angel. But it is the doing of good works that is the hallmark of humanity. It is in praise and service that the surprise of God is consummated.

—*Hildegard of Bingen*

Keys to FOURness

The energies of FOURness focus in the areas of organization, planning and achievement. To find your own relationship to FOURness, ask yourself the following questions:

1) As you consider your daily life, do you find that your life is mostly planned out ahead and that you have regular schedules and routines you follow?

2) Do you usually follow your calendar closely each day?

3) Is it important for you to set goals regularly in your life?

4) Is it a top priority for you to achieve excellence and do the task well?

5) Does your greatest enjoyment come from accomplishment?

6) Is it important for you to follow the rules and procedures?

7) Do you experience more pleasure whenever you are being useful?

8) Are you good at organizing chaos around you?

9) Do you tend to become suspicious of those who talk about their future dreams without working hard?

10) Do you enjoy working on different projects, perhaps often fixing and repairing things?

If you find that *yes* was your answer to most of these questions, it is likely that you are strongly connected to the stream of FOURness energy.

The Energy of FOURness
in World Symbolism

The ancient Pythagoreans proclaimed that FOUR is the greatest miracle. FOURness emanates the energies of organization and stability. It is the number of labor and work, which leads to solidity. The symbol of the square defines the boundaries of external manifestation on the physical plane.

FOUR signifies TWO meeting TWO. Man and woman meet each other as FOUR: the masculine and the feminine of the man meet the masculine and feminine of the woman. The psychologist C.G. Jung calls this aspect of FOURness the quaternity.

The energy of FOURness establishes the foundation for any undertaking. FOURness is the cornerstone that anchors the life of every person. Stability must always be established in the world of matter, so that the Great Law finds focus and a means for higher energies of Light to enter the world. Thus, every person's sincere effort and work opens doors for even greater results than we could imagine. Mundane activity in the world, which may often seem to be a struggle, is squared as it is permeated and filled with the Divine.

FOURness is the energy that pertains to the elements: fire, earth, air, and water. Likewise, the FOUR seasons, spring, summer, autumn, and winter, represent the cycles of nature that allow every person to work out God's Plan. FOURness energy also suggests the points of the compass—north, south, east, and west. San Marcos Square, in Venice, Italy, is the open square, where music is played antiphonally within the boundaries of FOUR corners. The Greeks mentioned the FOUR temperaments: choleric, sanguine, melancholic, and phlegmatic.

FOURness or 40 suggests the time needed to complete a process. FOUR, therefore, is a number that suggests fulfillment and the finishing of the task. Before Hitler, the Swastika, another symbol of FOURness, represented an emblem of good fortune, which described lines working themselves out to freedom and the triumph over matter. The fourth dimension of consciousness represents a higher way of seeing that takes sequential thinking and inspires it with new forms of intuition. In this way, FOURness reaches new perception through a "measuring intelligence that tabulates order."[1]

The Expression of FOURness in the Human Temperament

While the energies of THREEness release archetypes for artistic creativity, beauty, and imagination, the stream of FOURness emphasizes form and physical accomplishment. Energies released through FOURness find their primary focus in the physical body. Like the symbol of the square, the pathway of FOURness concentrates on structure, routine, planning, and scheduling. Inspiration now seeks concrete expression. People who are strongly attuned to the energy of FOURness are builders. Organized action grounds their desires and ideas, thus producing measurable gains and daily progress. What is ultimately important in FOURness is achieving durable results. Questions most asked by those who are motivated by the energy of FOURness would include the following:

- "Is it productive?"
- "Is it useful?"
- "Will it work?"
- "What do you expect to achieve?"
- "How long will it take?"

---

[1]G. Hodson, p. 147.

Attitudes and Behaviors of FOURness

People geared into the energy of FOURness always aim for excellence in performance. Doing the job well means finishing whatever they start—not quitting before seeing the assignment through to the end. Reliability and dependability are the essential ingredients of good workers. Although the task may not always be personally pleasing or enjoyable, it can be done willingly and diligently:

> In the course of one's life, it is not uncommon to be confronted with routine work which is not important for the advancement of the disciple's inward self. If this be your circumstance, remember it is then yours to do for the discipline and for the bringing forth of more willing service. Meditate on being a spokesman for the eternal at the point from which you serve.[2]

In the stream of FOURness, every minute counts. Time is valuable and must not be wasted:

> Dost thou love life?
> Then do not squander time,
> For that is the stuff life is made of.
>
> The sleeping fox catches no poultry.
> There will be sleeping enough in the grave.[3]

Theories, daydreams, fantasies and explanations count for something only if they produce results and constructive action. Satisfaction comes from the old refrain: "Well done, good and faithful servant." Fulfillment emerges from doing one's duty well and from love for one's work.

---

[2]F. A. Newhouse, *Disciplines of the Holy Quest* (Escondido, CA: Christward Ministry, 1959), pp. 103-4.
[3]B. Franklin, *Autobiography* (New York: Signet Classics, 1961), pp. 189-190.

The energy of FOURness deepens as people continue to develop their skills. Henry David Thoreau, the wise New England philosopher and lover of nature, pointed out the importance of improving the quality of one's life:

> I know of no more encouraging fact than the unquestionable ability of man to elevate his life by a conscious endeavor. . . . It is glorious to carve and paint the very atmosphere and medium through which we look, which morally we can do. To affect the quality of the day, that is the highest of the arts. Every man and woman are tasked to make their life even in its details, worthy of the contemplation of one's most elevated and critical hour.[4]

People strongly attuned to the path of FOURness live their lives with a planned daily structure. You will see them very much connected to daily schedules, goals and timelines. If they have a busy agenda, they will prioritize and do first what is most essential. They are efficiency-oriented, and they usually don't waste much time discussing feelings or demonstrating emotion. Because they place a strong emphasis on doing, it is very difficult for them to experience "free time." They tend to fill in empty periods with some new task or project.

Strengths from the Energy of FOURness

The following strengths emerge from the energy of FOURness: an ability to evaluate conditions and procedures, the capacity to formulate a plan and work for definite progress, an approach to problem-solving that is efficient and thorough, a talent for using time well, efficiency through routine, integrity and honesty by "dealing straight," and

---

[4]H. D. Thoreau, *Walden* (New York: Dodd, Mead & Co., 1946), p. 90.

an ability to do what is useful. People who demonstrate the power of FOURness are often mechanical and usually like to work with their hands. Even when not on the job, they like to tinker and improve objects. These people are compliant and reliable, and they see life pragmatically, with few frills. They admire precision.

Values and Creativity of FOURness

The power stream of FOURness highlights the following values and principles of life:

1) Steadfastness – the ability to keep on keeping on; maintaining your efforts, even in the midst of setbacks.

2) Endurance – the energy and willingness to withstand pressures and adversity.

3) Excellence – the capacity to do a job well, to the best of your abilities.

4) Integrity – being true to your word and doing what you say you will do; keeping your promises and doing what is required.

5) Honesty – fairness in your dealings with others; not taking advantage of others, especially when they are vulnerable.

6) Temperance – moderation and measure in all things.

7) Constancy – dependability and preparation over a long period of time; not "burning out" early.

8) Responsibility – the ability to respond.

The primary creativity for the person expressing the energy of FOURness lies in his or her ability to be productive. Eric Fromm, the great psychologist, describes productivity in these words: "One loves that for which one labors, and one labors for that which one loves."[5] In this way, the person who expresses the energy of FOURness is the salt of the earth.

A common motto for the expression of FOURness is, "Do it, think it, and feel it." Creativity emerges out of a systematic approach to life, a decency and a tenacity that does not waver. In this approach a person will tend to see life sequentially, one step at a time. Regularity and being conscientious provide competency. Through effort, it is possible to improve conditions that once may have been unglamorous. From childhood, a person who is strongly connected to the energy of FOURness will demonstrate a strong capacity for self-discipline and loyalty. Such an individual will respect hard work and honest effort; he or she will agree with the words of the psychologist Alfred Adler:

> A man or woman of genius
> is primarily a person of
> supreme usefulness.[6]

In my counseling work, it is always a marvel how people who may be quite different in their approaches to life come together and affect each other. It is clear that the nine great energy streams circulate through each of us in different proportions, according to our consciousness and receptivity. However, each stream, with its unique energies, can feed the others. I remember counseling two young children. Jane was a true romantic, very artistic and

---

[5]E. Fromm, *The Art of Loving* (New York: Harper & Row, 1956), p. 27.
[6]A. Adler, *What Life Should Mean to You* (New York: Perigree Book, 1958), p. 9.

very casual—strongly centered in the energy stream of THREEness. Her brother, David, was already an organizer, a high achiever in school, and very industrious— already an advocate for the energy of FOURness. When bedtime came, David would carefully close the books on his desk and arrange them in his bag to take to school the next morning; he would carefully place his shoes by his bed, ready to put on when he got up. His day was already organized, with very little prompting from his parents.

Jane was a different tone altogether. She related to her homework when she felt "inspired," her colorful school bag rarely had the right books in it, and her shoes often were left in the livingroom, under the couch, or in a chair, where she had been listening to music or drawing. Yet love blossomed between Jane and David: he would put his arm around her, gently reminding her about her schoolwork, and she would play her flute for him in between his assignments. Fortunately, their parents understood their ways and their needs. They respected the essential strengths of each child and tried to help Jane and David fill in what was less familiar and more difficult. At one point they were able to get Jane to write herself "reminder notes" on brightly colored paper—and she was better at finding her toothbrush. They also made sure that David went to the movies once a month and took time just to have fun. Thus, the Law of Compensation, which is always vital in any relationship or household, was active in that family.

Observing the Spectrum of FOURness Energy

The energy of FOURness tends to emerge the most clearly during grade school. This is an important stage of childhood development, when young persons build their skills and find models for their heroes. It is a time of industry and achievement, the keynotes of the pathway of FOUR-ness. Carefully chosen, encouraging words coming from parents, teachers, police officers, coaches, ministers, and other advocates can release strong energies and burgeoning talents. It is also a time for building goals and organizing plans. If FOURness energy, positively directed, is freely expressed during the approximate ages of 6 to 11, a good foundation for future direction and focused accomplishment is often insured. If there is confusion and little incentive, and if opportunities to achieve are few, it may be difficult for a child to bring out FOURness in a positive, productive expression. Laziness, lack of thoroughness, and poor self-worth can be the resulting behaviors and attitudes.

In a different way, too much emphasis upon work, keeping busy, super achievement, and excessive structure to each day can cause responses that become robotic and non-feeling. Needless nagging and workaholic expectations can cause some people to be too tied to the task and uptight if they do not have some project to finish. For such people who exhibit the behaviors of excessive FOURness, it seems to them that no matter how much they do, it is never good enough.

The Underdeveloped Expression of FOURness (–4)

There is little sense of any plan or focus.
Procrastination is frequent.
There is a dislike of hard physical work and long hours.
A tendency to quit early, before the job is finished, prevails.
The work is not done thoroughly; results are non-productive.
Advice is resisted.
The person dislikes following the plan or the rules.
The life remains uncommitted.

Procedures are ignored.

It is easy to dawdle away the hours.

Undisciplined efforts lead to fruitlessness.

Passive-resistant behaviors prevent progress and completion.

The person remains "out to lunch."

Motivation is poor and lacks direction or purposefulness.

Intentionality waits in the wings.

The person does not enjoy definite structure or concreteness.

Promises are soon forgotten.

No routine or regularity is present.

"Whatever!"

The person remains forever talented but unskilled.

Lack of organization just "lets it slide."

Stability is not sufficient to produce achievement.

The Balanced Expression of FOURness (4)

The warrior finishes the task.

Real laborers always try to do their best.

The person thrives on hard work and purposeful activity.

Achievement involves applying oneself to the task at hand.

Be vigilant and demonstrate loyalty and compliance.

Be a good provider; prove dependability.

The person is able to endure and maintains the effort.

Set standards; follow the rules, codes and regulations.

Live with integrity and "cut the mustard."

Temperance is preferable.

Become self-reliant.

Establish a framework and a method. Be a builder!

Build the foundation; make the form visible.

Maintain regularity and be systematic in your approach.

"Four-squared, the city stands."

Produce results and look at life pragmatically.

Follow traditional ways and customs.
Life is made up of "nuts and bolts."
Find the anchor and be well-grounded.
Ideas must be implemented to become useful.
Value excellence and performance.
Roll up the sleeves and dig in!
A reliable person becomes the "salt of the earth."
Remain conscientious and be honest.
Something is valid when it works and is useful.
It is always necessary to be decent.
Always "play by the book."

The Excessive Expression of FOURness (+4)

Life becomes too regimented and "boxed in."
Issues become too cut and dried.
The person is too literal and boring.
Workaholic attitudes prevent relaxation and cover up feelings.
Dogmatic, inflexible and sceptical responses kill others' dreams.
Rigidity dampens spontaneity. Life becomes too mechanical.
The person may be prejudiced and hidebound.
Life becomes too linear and sequential and is lived only "by the book."
Resistance and denial make one stubborn like a mule.
The "ramrod" becomes unbendable.
Sternness and severity keep the person insensitive to others' needs.
There is no room for deviation from any plan or rules.
Commitments and duties become overwhelming and exhausting.
"I am loved only for what I do." Always keep busy!
Responses are too deliberate, and life becomes a "heavyweight."

Too much predictability makes life a monotone.
Obsessed with the work, the person becomes emotionally
    phlegmatic.
One can become stifled by self-imposed procedures and
    time frames.
Limited opinions and perspective reveal a bigot.
The person becomes too "square" and uptight.
Feelings are frozen and are replaced by robot-like
    behavior.
Burnout is the logical outcome.
Life is never mellow.
The person is a perpetual over-achiever who can never do
    enough.

Case Study in the Energies of FOURness

The following case study is about a man who learned how
to temper his excessive FOURness, which manifested as
fear of intimacy and frozen feelings. Mr. M. was an excellent provider for his family. He would often work long
hours, supposedly because his family "needed the
money," but the earnings would always be spent on his
terms, for "sensible" necessities, such as extra toilet paper
and cans of oil for future "lube jobs" on the cars. Mean-
while, young Teddy, the son, began to get into trouble at
school. When he broke into a neighbor's home and stole
some cigarettes, the matter became serious enough for
Dad to come home early and "have a talk with his boy." It
was the first time that Dad had made it home for supper in
more than two months. Mr. M. resented the inconvenience of having to come home "early"—the traffic at 5:00
P.M. was much heavier than at 9:00 P.M. The father's talk
with Teddy was short and sweet: "We don't put up with
stealing in this house; go to your room; there will be no
more baseball for two months."

The stealing continued. Suddenly, Dad's job mysteriously ended. He found a position closer to home, allowing him to be with his son more. For two weekends everything changed: Dad took Teddy to the ballgame and to the ocean. Teddy's attitude began to change; he became more friendly and less sullen. Then Dad "saw a need" at work, and he offered to work extra and stay late. The long hours returned, Dad was again an absentee parent, and one day Teddy was arrested and taken to the police station for taking drugs. Dad didn't know what more to do, and he persisted in pointing out and lecturing Teddy about how hard he worked for the family. When the family was assigned to counseling, Dad finally got the message: he saw how little closeness and affection he had received as a boy; his own father was away long hours and rarely spoke to him except to criticize. When he did relate with his father, Mr. M. remembered sadly that it was almost always through a task or an order, never just talking, sharing or expressing feelings.

Mr. M. never could do the job well enough for his own dad, so he always tried to do more, hoping that some day it might prove sufficient. But it never was. Mr. M.'s dad died without ever telling his son that he loved him, just for himself. His last words were, "Be sure to do a good job; don't be lazy, the way you are." With this programming, it was very difficult for Dad to be there now for Teddy. Frozen feelings and a fear of inadequacy made Mr. M. increasingly unavailable to a son who loved his dad and just wanted to be near and friendly.

It is amazingly true to realize, "Whatever you did not adequately receive in your own childhood may be the greatest gift you will be required to give to others." Our children, being highly intuitive, tune in immediately to our blind spots and unresolved issues. They often become the stimulus to help us work through our imbalances. They activate our connection with the nine great streams of energy that eventually provide the needed balances and solutions to our lives. When we resist or refuse to work through our issues, our children take in (introjection) and act out what is weak, denied, or "unborn" in us. As the writer, Anne Wilson Schaef, points out:

> In many families when children feel and express their feelings, the family is forced to deal with its own reality. If children are helped to express their feelings and explore them, they lose their fear of feelings and can find out what the feeling—whether it is sadness, fear or joy—is all about.[7]

Expanding the Energy of FOURness

1) Make a commitment today to finish at least one unfinished task or project. Set a timeline and a final date.

2) Make one promise and keep it.

3) For one week, plan each day on the calendar. Try to follow the plan as much as possible.

4) Before going to bed each night, list four accomplishments for the day. They don't have to be enormous.

5) List your achievements to date. What do you want to achieve within the next year? Within the next five years?

6) Find at least four ways that you can build better routine into your day.

7) Evaluate the daily rituals in your life: how much do you take part in such things as walking the dog, jogging, reading the newspaper, watching certain television

---

[7]A. W. Schaef, p. 74.

programs, driving a certain road to a certain place, etc.? If you have no regularity in your life, you may begin with something as small as eating a meal for one week at the same, designated hour, with your family or pet.

8) What do you enjoy fixing? What improvements are you planning around the house, in your job, on your automobile, etc.?

 The Energy of FIVEness

Personal love . . . and the essence of falling in love is a sudden collapse of a section of an individual's ego boundaries, permitting one to merge his or her identity with that of another person. . . . The experience of merging with a loved one has in it echoes from the time when we were merged with our mothers in infancy.

—*M. Scott Peck*

Man is a natural gambler, and life is the biggest stake he can lay. The greater the odds, the greater the thrill. . . . The greatness of sensation is mutual; . . . I am true to the promptings of the life that is in me.

—*Jack London*

Keys to FIVEness

The energies of FIVEness focus in areas such as freedom, variety and physical sensation. To discover your own connection with the stream of FIVEness, answer the following questions:

1) Do you take time to exercise your body each day? (This does not mean just going to work or doing a task.)
2) Is it enjoyable to you to touch other people who are attractive to you?
3) Are you a good hugger?
4) Do you need lots of freedom and space to move?
5) Do you continuously have many irons in the fire?
6) Is it easy for you to be spontaneous, such as accepting a sudden invitation to dine out?
7) Do you get easily irritated when life crowds you?
8) Is it easy for you to be persuasive and convincing with others?
9) Do you thrive on variety, travel, and continuous change?
10) In general do you find bodies interesting?

If you have answered *yes* to most of the questions, you are strongly connected to the power of FIVEness.

The Energy of FIVEness in World Symbolism

In the symbolism of numbers, FIVEness stands midway between ONEness and NINEness. Shaped somewhat like a rocking chair, FIVE is an energy that is continuously in motion, oscillating between extremes, and finding balance by relating many peripheral activities and interests to the central focus. We can visualize a five-pointed star, glistening outward toward different points of contact, then drawing the energy back, to the center of the star. Thus, the energy of FIVEness becomes the number of life experience, becoming flexible and finding focus in the midst of variety and extremity. It is catharsis—an emptying that releases tension.

Being the midpoint between ONEness and NINEness, FIVEness becomes a "mediator" of life's processes; it is an energy that continuously rearranges natural conditions in ways that bring freedom from limitation and new openings. FIVEness seeks some impersonal root in demonstrating the operations of law and the many expressions of the life force.[1]

FIVEness represents humanity; "man is the only species that stands erect, with the cerebrum poised at right angles to the spine; the only species that utilizes two limbs from the function of locomotion for the exclusive service of the mind and brain; the only species in which the segments of the spine are the measures of the angles of the cube; the only species with a spoken, recorded language, an alphabet, a recorded history and a prospective future."[2]

The energy of FIVEness is filled with multiple options: FIVEness reaches Godward, toward the heavens, and it reaches down into the earth. In the array of FIVEness, the earthy base supports a divine longing. With the legs planted on the ground, head and arms reach skyward.

In many ancient writings, FIVEness is related to medicine and suggests the purification process of the body. It is thus a symbol of healing and sanitation; it signifies cleansing of the body temple.

---

[1]G. Hodson, p. 147.
[2]F. H. & H. Curtiss, *The Voice of Isis*, p. 366.

Islam suggests FIVEness in the teaching of the Articles of Belief: Allah, Angels, the prophet, predestination and the day of judgment.

The Expression of FIVEness in the Human Temperament

Whereas the energy of FOURness uses the physical body to work for concrete results and the organization of forms, the power of FIVEness circulates through the physical body like a sudden, electrical charge providing excitement and sensation. For FIVEness, life is a playground of perpetually new experiences. The stream of FIVEness highlights the keynotes of freedom and movement. The motto is, "Don't fence me in!" FIVEness needs plenty of room physically to move and explore; people attuned to FIVEness may easily become irritated if they are confined or limited.

Desires on the path of FIVEness are usually physical. Many meetings that occur may be only brief encounters, but they are often explosive in the moment. Appetites are intensified. As Abraham Maslow, the psychologist, once remarked, "Man is perpetually a wanting animal." Sudden contact, deep release, satiation and moving on mark is the pattern of FIVEness.

People who taste the flavors of FIVEness often crave instant gratification more than long-term commitments. For a brief time there may be strong attraction and total immersion of oneself in another, much like a consuming fire or a surging wave. But such intensity cannot be sustained for long periods; burnout, collapse and exhaustion soon occur, with a certain feeling of recoil and emptiness.

The energy of FIVEness is highly kinetic. People expressing FIVEness are usually "in transit," on the move, heading on, somewhere else. It is difficult to hold their attention; their eyes dart everywhere. They usually have many irons in the fire; they discharge energy with an intensity, their movements are rapid, often herky-jerky, as though they were on fire. They would gladly agree with the Greek philosopher, Heraclitus, who said that the only thing permanent in life is change. The way of FIVEness is movement; FIVEness expresses the need to discharge energy continuously as a means of resisting inertia. In truth, each of us, at different times and places in our life, revolts against the status quo or the feeling of limitation. FIVEness releases energy continuously through the body—its muscles, tendons, joints, and nervous system—in an effort to move ahead into newness.

The power of FIVEness is most effective when movement knows its limits and its timing. Like the five-pointed star, FIVEness moves out like arrows of energy in many different directions; it must also learn to bring that energy back into some central focus, so that some productivity is possible. It is easy on this path to squander one's efforts or to find in later life that many different outlets and interests have yielded too many unfinished ventures and a life of scatteredness. Continuity becomes more valuable than mere shortcuts.

Attitudes and Behaviors of FIVEness

Since physical contact and touch are essential for people strong in the energies of FIVEness, they often enjoy contact sports; dancing that is vigorous; exercise and body-building programs; martial arts; health and diet programs; and outdoor activities, such as camping, hiking, mountain climbing, and travel. Frequently, sex is a high priority. These people show a definite interest in bodies—body watching, body shapes, sizes, smells, fashion and modeling, massage, "pumping iron," shaping their limbs, better fitness, as well as showing a curiosity about the parts of the anatomy and how they work.

I remember a workshop that I participated in once. I shared the program with a strong FIVEness advocate. The evening was planned for two parts: the first would explore healthy relationships from a physical point of view, and I was to speak about sensitivity and understanding afterward. Mr. E. began by going into the anatomy of the reproductive organs, showing various pictures with great interest and animation. He then moved into a breathtaking fantasy about how rare it is for conception to occur and how intimately the sperm and egg meet each other. His talk gathered momentum, until two hours later all participants were perspiring, exhausted yet visibly moved. He had made a real drama out of the activities of sexual organs, and everyone undoubtedly felt moved. My part, which followed, was quite anti-climactic and tame by comparison. I'll never forget how all the attendants at that workshop breathed heavily as they went out into the night. Later, alone with me, Mr. E. continued with more material on vibrators, health foods, aphrodisiacs, such as sarsaparilla and carrots, and acupuncture points. He confessed to me as we parted that for him life was a perpetual playground of sensation and delight.

The nature of FIVEness energy is exploratory, experimental and often transitory. People strongly expressing this energy are likely to enjoy high risk, visceral release, and ceaseless vitality. There is a continuous need to discharge tension and restlessness. Children cannot sit still for long periods in school; they need to get up and move around. Often, the behaviors are more reckless, instinctive and impulsive, fiery, and unconventional. Usually, exhaustion is the only hope for quiet and stillness. They need a lot of room and open space.

People releasing energy through the stream of FIVEness are versatile and highly persuasive. A primary interest is the adventure of "making the sale," and often a strong "hype" and "attractive packaging" become convincing in the moment. These individuals are flexible and adaptable. They meet the public very easily and can roll with the punches. Life is primarily promotional: a large repertoire of verbal strategies and a pitch from every angle overcome many temporary obstacles. These people often get quick flashes of insight; they play their hunches and go for the lucky roll and the winning hand. A quick gesture, accompanied by suggestive body language, and the momentary offer of a "real bargain" will often bring the deal to a successful close. There may be some exaggeration and bragging.

As the energy of ONEness implodes with the mind, FIVEness often welds together several strands and sources of perspective into a sudden blaze of power—much like sparks of white heat shot from an anvil or a shooting star. When this blitz of energy hits its target, a strong, explosive moment activates behaviors and outcomes.

A continuous enthusiasm and a hearty love of life sparkle from people expressing the energy of FIVEness. They are spontaneous, fun-loving, full of earthy (even ribald) humor and practical jokes. Excitement and loud laughter accompany them wherever they go. Risqué memories often seem to surface in the midst of an energy flow that most resembles a juggler: quick laughter, running to the restroom, sudden phone call to "check out" a lead, scratching an itch, catching a falling object, then quickly exiting into the rainy night, leaving in the memory a sound of screeching tires and a flashing red light. These people leave us breathless; they live several lifetimes in one, they are always "into new interests," and they rebound quickly from continuous bumps and collisions, only to surface somewhere else. If they feel that they are being confined or limited, energy may suddenly be discharged, like a thunderstorm. But take a few breaths, and such temper tantrums are usually quickly gone, and the traveler is eager to move on to the next exciting episode.

These people realize that it is better to release irritation quickly; harboring it is a waste of time and can be injurious.

The energy of FIVEness is never predictable or orthodox. In fact, there is usually no pattern at all for very long. Form has less meaning and may often be destroyed as the greater vitality of the Presence is released. The energy of FIVEness is random, aleatoric, and eccentric, without regular limits or structure, rarely sustaining a definite direction, and always bringing some twist or novelty. A life lived in the spirit of FIVEness energy can become a perpetual "trip," filled with endless reversals, variety, and the need for continuous alertness. As David Spangler, futuristic thinker, has indicated, "Peace is life . . . abundantly overflowing its limitations."[3] The sheer motion and energy of FIVEness keeps everything in circulation.

It is often difficult for people strongly attuned to the energy of FIVEness to fit in or find easy acceptance. Because of their kinetic energy and rapid movements, the world may often tend to see them as bizarre or even dangerous. Sometimes, in between episodes, these people may feel disconnected, panicky, and cut off from the mainstream of life. Because they may be doing many things simultaneously, others may not always know what to do with them. Thus, being unable to label or categorize a person displaying the varied lifestyle of FIVEness energy, others might not even acknowledge that such an individual exists. It's as though the rapid energy of certain persons keeps them invisible and undefinable.

It is also important for this type to realize some depth in the midst of their variety. They may not finish much of what they start, but it is essential that they complete something regularly. Parents of such children must thread their balance by not being too demanding, but they do well to

---

[3]D. Spangler, *Revelation* (San Francisco, CA: Rainbow Bridge, 1976), p. 75.

insist that at least one out of five interests be carried to a conclusion. Most children's self-esteem increases, even in the midst of protests and impatient cries of boredom, if they can accomplish as well as experience. If they fail to finish something too often, they can easily become too fragmented in their behaviors. Repeated break-ups in jobs, relationships, and interests can lead to feelings of defeat, frustration, remorse, and even deteriorization in physical health. As these young people move on in life, it is disenchanting to find that they have burned all their bridges, and no continuity is visible. The need for some sense of meaning surfaces as they consider distant memories of cheap thrills and one-night stands. Loneliness and disillusionment may set in during later life, when they sense little evidence of depth or meaningful achievement. The last stage of life may result in cynical, pessimistic feelings about existence. Rebellion gives way to despair.

Because people of FIVEness tend to be wilder, extreme, and combustible, they are wise to "stay within their energy field." They benefit by learning to conserve some of their energy, rather than discharging too much in fits and spurts. They do well to take care of their physical body:

> Every person is responsible for his own body as the temple for the new mysteries; he must prepare it by cleansing the blood through appropriate diet, correct breathing, training and meditation. The body must become an organ through which the light and fire of the spirit can work to overcome the darkness of our environment.[4]

4G. Trevelyan, *A Vision of the Aquarian Age* (Walpole, NH: 1984), p. 73.

Strengths from the Energy of FIVEness

Certain strengths are released through the energy of FIVEness. They are as follows: versatility, physical prowess, spontaneity, the ability to gather a wealth of new experiences, resourcefulness, bodily alertness, and the ability to keep life exciting and have adventure. The essence of FIVEness is freedom and playfulness.

Values and Creativity of FIVEness

These are the outstanding values and creative aspects of FIVEness:

1) Enthusiasm and Vitality—the capacity to be filled with the Spirit.

2) Adaptability—willingness to make continuous adjustments in the midst of rapid challenges and demanding situations.

3) Good Humor—ability to laugh, even at oneself.

In the fields of creativity, the energy of FIVEness vibrates with those jobs and interests that offer constant change and newness: chauffeur, travel agent, stewardess, caterer, interviewer, sales representative, detective, promoter, advertiser, runner, courier, delivery person, announcer, photographic journalist, speculator, agent, and animal care. These people enjoy bouncing off the great, ongoing spectacle of life that is often found in shopping malls, sports arenas, stadiums, circuses, and cavalcades. All of these offer endless kinetic combinations of color, shape, and size. Individuals who are strongly connected to the stream of FIVEness often find their best insights while driving or on the go. They make good huggers, not cuddlers, and they need to pace themselves, remaining in touch with their own body rhythms:

> The proportions of the body are as the harmonies of music, and are reflected again in the great edifices of worship. . . . If man is indeed the microcosm reflecting and embodying the macrocosm, then within the miracle of the body must be enshrined all the secrets of the universe.[5]

Observing the Spectrum of FIVEness Energy

Because one of the main themes of FIVEness is the need for physical stimulation, sensation, and appetite, issues of addiction and co-dependence tend to center primarily around the physical body. Often, as a child, the individual strongly connected to the energy of FIVEness may undergo issues relating to physical abuse, violence in the household, "rage-aholic" parents, sexual, alcohol, and drug abuse, eating disorders, sexual dysfunctions, accidents and collisions (from too much confusion), and reckless behavior, such as drunk driving, that goes against the social system of law and order.

Children who are strongly expressing the energy of FIVEness are often misunderstood: they are basically kinetic and need to move around much of the day. They cannot be expected to sit still for very long, and they need outlets, such as sports, gymnastics, and the out of doors — nature release. Parents and teachers who may be more structured frequently mistake such children as being hyperactive, sometimes called "Attention Deficit Disorder." Such children will usually cooperate, but they are very unconventional and live more "in the moment." They

---

[5]G. Trevelyan, p. 86.

may "strike out" suddenly—in frustration—or they may seem rebellious or "maverick" because they are so quick and verbally honest. In family situations, they frequently play the "rebel" role, always seeming to go against the family order and finding it difficult to conform, to follow rules or adhere to society's ways. This tendency may accelerate as they reach adolescence. It is very important for these individuals to be taught early the basic ways of society and family. It is helpful, for example, to introduce such children to the Scouts and other community functions. In this way the many gifts and versatility of FIVEness can learn to interact appropriately with the social order in activities and behaviors that are not self-defeating or alienating.

If the energy of FIVEness is impeded or too confined, frustration sets in. Excessive behaviors result in hedonism, promiscuity, renegade-ism, vulgarity, hot-head responses and temper outbursts, Dionysian excess in areas of sex and eating, scheming and general recklessness. Often, the turmoil of irritability and "hit first—talk later" distortions replace a more reasonable, sensitive approach. Those who are excessively FIVE in their energy are also too curious about the more lurid byways of life: they may fall into the "peep show" consciousness of destructive fascination:

> Fascination is an ambivalent emotion in which the attraction is enhanced by the concomitant repulsion. It arouses the instincts and appeals to the lower passions; it excites by its sensual enchantment.[6]

Too much excitement and confusion tend to weaken those expressing the distorted unbalanced sides of FIVEness. Burnout and "spinning one's wheels" can be

---

[6]R. Assagioli, *Psychosynthesis* (New York: Viking Press, 1965), p. 243.

avoided through better time management and some planning. Radical and "kinky" behaviors, plus a manic life style, can lead to illness and fatal overdose. FIVEness, in its highest expression, can be interesting, exciting and stimulating, without carrying eccentricity and extremism too far. The spectrum of FIVEness can be described in the following way.

The Underdeveloped Expression of FIVEness (–5)

The body is treated prudishly.
Avoidance of touching and physical affection is preferred.
There is a fear of spontaneity.
Life exists without any fun.
Travel and variety are not desired.
The person is uninformed sexually.
Only certain things are acceptable.
Information about bodily health is often quite limited.
There is resistance to new impressions and new approaches.
Exercise comes only in work, never for sensation or pleasure.
Interests are few.
Each day is lived as predictably as possible.
The person refuses to change habits.
Never take a fling or try something for adventure.
Vacations and times of recreation and renewal are rare.

The Balanced Expression of FIVEness (5)

Freedom, variety, and newness are the most exciting parts of life.
It is fun to be playful and intriguing; difficult to take a stand.

Sudden changes are frequent. Feelings of pressure are likely to be intense at certain moments.

Keep many irons in the fire; try to keep as many hot as possible.

Be adaptable and flexible.

"Tasters" discard and rebound easily. "Longterm" is more difficult.

Seize the moment, enjoy sensation and appetites, and look for instant gratification.

Curiosity and exploration open new doors in life.

Relieve tensions by diversifying your energies.

Earthy jokes and clowning are a "blast."

The "right" sales pitch scores quickly and wins new fans.

Promotional "wheeling and dealing" is often persuasive in the moment.

A certain friction keeps life unpredictable, on the cutting edge.

"Keep life moving" and be willing to experiment. Become versatile!

Improvise quickly, like a juggler doing a balancing act.

Unorthodox approaches are preferable. The person enjoys playing devil's advocate.

Relationships may mean contacts on the run.

"Get the scoop!" Each person becomes an item.

When pressured, the person is able to "scramble" well.

Frequent mood swings make the person seem like a rocking chair; the challenge is to keep stable.

Current fashion and display are alluring.

Look for shortcuts! Cash in quickly!

Make your own rules as you go along.

Physical contact is powerful and combustible, always visceral.

The body wants to be kinetic and incessantly on the go.

Spurts and flurries of activity are seldom long lasting.

Behaviors exhibit a certain fierceness at times.

The Excessive Expression of FIVEness (+5)

Compulsive and addictive behaviors are a way to release feelings or to escape from feelings.

Excessive, "out of control" behaviors provide euphoria or an altered mood state.

Life is too chaotic and reckless, often frantic and erratic.

The energy is too scattered, and the person is too easily distracted.

Attention span is too limited; person cannot sustain direction.

Passions erupt, and exhaustion is likely to follow.

Tempers flare easily, especially if limits are imposed and enforced.

Too many ventures, abandoned prematurely, keep life episodic and unfulfilling.

Angry, frustrated responses often lead to physical violence and abuse.

Deviant, "kinky" behavior is frequent.

Language may be coarse and vulgar. Crudeness is common.

Constant feeding of an appetite results in overdose and never "getting enough."

Sudden reactions may be "radical" and inappropriate.

Any impingement on freedom results in eruptive defiance and rebellious behaviors.

The person has difficulty staying within his own energy field.

Life goes "off the board" or out of bounds.

Too much high speed becomes reckless and causes collisions.

If something doesn't come easily, there is little patience or follow-through.

Many opportunities are abandoned and become "throw-aways."

Tantrums are frequent. Impulsive responses are typical.

The life style is too irregular and lacks any real depth.
Spending sprees may be one of many binges for newness.
Boredom and the need for sensation are repeatedly present.
Sexual promiscuity and carelessness may lead to diseases and many broken relationships.
It is thrilling to court danger and disaster.
Too much playing with fire results in getting burned.
Under pressure, the person panics and "splits."
Craving is uncontrolled. The energy is too spasmodic.
The person is always restless and on the go.
Others may become mere toys and amusements.
Constant commotion is typical.

Case Studies in the Energies of FIVEness

Mr. A. typifies the positive energies of FIVEness. He radiates energy and vitality as he races from place to place. He has several professions: he is an outstanding hypnotherapist, with a stream of daily appointments, including children and adults of all ages. In between appointments, Mr. A. rushes out to check on sales and progress of his bookstore, which he coordinates. After his appointments end, Mr. A. sets up for his evening group, called "Codependency Recoverers Anonymous," an array of people who come to share and progress beyond their difficulties. Upon arriving home later, Mr. A. continues his project to provide stress-reduction tapes for court reporters. He works an hour on his computer and records some interesting data. At present he is working on a book, geared to help overcome negative parental conditioning from childhood. Whenever a client cannot keep an appointment, Mr. A. immediately shifts gears and finds another person to fit in, or he opens his black, magical bag and extracts a new file containing cryptic notes or a tape that describes a new, exciting project. At present Mr. A. is working with a teacher in the public schools to provide hypnotherapeutic-musical relaxation tapes for emotionally disturbed children; he is also building on an addition to his home, he is re-editing tapes for his wife, who is an excellent instructor in esoteric studies, he is taking his grandson out to a movie, or he is getting ready for the next festival of the arts, which gathers many musicians and artisans and authors for a day of celebration and sales. Mr. A. personifies FIVEness: a whirlwind of energy, always new, exciting, dynamic, pleasant, on the run, and filled with enthusiasm.

Expanding the Energy of FIVEness

1) Find ways to bring more variety into your life. Add some new interests and activities for pleasure and enjoyment.

2) Join a club or a toastmaster's group; speak to new groups of people.

3) Read a newspaper or magazine that keeps you up-to-date about current affairs and global happenings.

4) Interview someone about his or her life and what he or she has experienced. Learn by asking some of the following questions:

   • How have you handled your temper?
   • What do you do when you get angry?
   • How do you handle your feelings of boredom?
   • What do you feel about sex?
   • How do you care for your body?

5) Begin to walk some each day, perhaps building to one to two miles a day. Breathe in good air; release tensions.

6) Take a trip, even a short one, regularly. Change the scenery.

7) Do one thing different each day.

8) Move your body more—investigate swimming, stretching, dancing.

9) Take a beginner's course in acupressure, "Touch for Health," or foot reflexology.

10) Learn more about diet and good nutrition.

11) Learn more about how your body functions. Try to feel the sensations and "body language" more.

12) Did you give and receive at least one hug today?

13) Develop your sense of taste by trying some new foods and recipes.

14) Treat yourself to a therapeutic body massage; enjoy it!

15) Read the book, *Bio Energetics*, by Alexander Lowen.

The
Energy
of
SIXness

All friendship implies a certain degree of communion; a certain likeness must exist between friends, [some] essential community of interests. . . . Friendship is essentially generous. If friendship is to transpire between two [or more] people, it is important that both be in a state of availability. . . . It is in and by friendship that we experience ourselves. . . . We make the life of a friend ours with the most total respect for his or her otherness. . . . The creative activity of friends is borne by their common hope, by their common involvement in the service of the transcendent. [In the midst of] its imperfections and limitations . . ., friendship represents one of the most precious values of the human condition.

—*Ignace Lepp*

Keys to SIXness

The stream of SIXness focuses on the themes of family, group and community. Home and nurturing are important interests of those who express the energies of SIXness. To see how strongly you may be connected to this stream of energy, consider these questions:

1) Do you enjoy helping and nurturing others regularly?

2) Are you frequently involved in social programs and causes?

3) Do you enjoy spending a lot of time with your family and relatives?

4) Are you closely bonded with your parents?

5) Even if it inconveniences you, do you enjoy taking time to help someone?

6) Do you regularly celebrate family traditions, such as birthdays, anniversaries, graduations, weddings and reunions?

7) Is it important for you to be around people regularly?

8) Are your friends an important part of your life?

9) Is it important for you to be noticed and accepted by others?

10) Do you socialize frequently and go to parties and outings?

The more questions you answered with *yes*, the more strongly you are linked to the energies of SIXness.

The Energy of SIXness in World Symbolism

Whereas FIVEness is generative, SIXness is regenerative. Procreation is followed by many hours of caring and rearing. After the child is born, the nurturing energies of SIXness need to be constant. Thus, SIXness, often considered to be the number of marriage, home and family, domesticates the personal, passionate, impregnating moments of FIVEness. SIXness is warmth; SIXness is the hearth. The seed, once planted, must be nurtured.

The work of creation was completed "in SIX days," and the Chinese say, "SIX Breaths produced all things in silence."[1] SIXness thus indicates labor and service with deep loving feeling; SIXness was dedicated by Pythagoras to Venus, the goddess of human love. SIXness is beauty and emanates the luminous soul quality of kindness. SIXness is an archetype for humanity, connected by a common caring.

SIXness describes the group energy, networking and helping together. Group activity is powerful, like the anthill: "Go to the ant, thou sluggard; consider her ways and be wise."[2]

There is an inner, esoteric and exalted dimension to SIXness: caring for others leads a person into greater powers and spiritual openings. The honorary 33 degree in Freemasonry signifies completion and fulfillment of one's responsibilities; in a person there are 33 (reducing to 6 — 3 + 3) vertebrae "protecting the spinal canal through which the transmuted life forces pass from the lower, sexual chakra to the higher faculties in the head."[3] Esoterically, Jacob's Ladder represents this vertebral column and 33 steps toward higher consciousness. These 33 steps

---

[1] C. Heline, p. 46.
[2] Proverbs 6:6.
[3] C. Heline, p. 50.

toward spiritual completeness are mentioned by one spiritual teacher[4] as:

> . . . lead[ing] one to spiritual enlightenment and mastery. It is important that we consciously strive to take as many of these steps as we can this lifetime:

1. Reverence for God

2. Reverence for Christ

3. Reverence for the Holy Ones of God

4. Purification

5. Gratitude

6. Spiritual Purposefulness

7. Responsibility

8. Development and Increase of Spiritual Trust

9. Regular Times for Meditation and Prayer

10. The Quest for and Right Use of Knowledge

11. Respect for the Day at Hand

12. Unfoldment of Our Higher Nature

13. Accurate Truthfulness

14. Unselfishness

15. Spiritual Love

---

[4]The extract and the list that follows, giving 33 steps to spiritual enlightenment, come from F. A. Newhouse, *Quest Lessons* (Escondido, CA: Christward Ministry), vol. I, pp. 238–239.

16. Universality

17. Humility

18. Cheerfulness

19. Courage

20. Compassion

21. Self-Control

22. Patience

23. Teachableness

24. Poise

25. Industriousness

26. Intelligence

27. Objectivity

28. Daily Growth

29. Overcoming Ego

30. Overcoming Fear

31. Overcoming Envy

32. Overcoming Prejudice

33. Overcoming Littleness

Thus, SIXness leads ultimately into the heavenly rooms of God's House.

SIXness signifies beauty, loveliness, and harmony in action. It is the mind dedicated to caring and service. SIXness is the culmination of social service and mission to humanity. After SIX, one goes forward, no longer remaining tied to any one family, group, or community. According to the Pythagoreans, SIXness is the perfection of parts; SIXness coordinates the FIVE fingers of the hand and the FIVE toes of the foot with the love of the heart. SIXness is benevolence.

According to the Theosophical writer, Geoffrey Hodson, SIXness expresses a mutual link, reciprocal activity, counterpoise, complementary efforts, a harmony of opposites, the psyche's interaction of the spiritual, material, mental, and physical energies in each person.[5]

Homer Curtiss, another Theosophical writer, describes SIXness as primarily the number of Nature. It is "the number of the Christ principle, but only as it pertains to the manifestation of Christ's Universal Power in Nature."[6] The geometrical symbol of SIXness is the Star of David, two interlaced triangles, the divine and human natures interlinking with equipoise and balanced symmetry.

The Expression of SIXness in the Human Temperament

While the energy of FIVEness views life as an exciting adventure, the power of SIXness emerges as the nurturing and caring for others. The energy of SIXness is warm, emotional, and strong in "people needing people." Mottos for SIXness include, "Count on me," and "Lend a hand."

It is rare to find people strong in SIXness alone. They are usually with peers or family, sharing a cup of coffee, tea, or playing cards or board games. Their relationships are most often "true blue." In such homes, people may come together to watch television, discuss books or community events, eat together, or set up local programs and fund drives. Dinners, concerts, plays, and other social-

[5]G. Hodson, p. 148.
[6]F. H. & H. Curtiss, *The Voice of Isis*, p. 367.

artistic functions occur often. The primary emphasis, at its best, is sociability. Sometimes these meetings may lead to deeper learning.

Attitudes and Behaviors of SIXness

People on the path of SIXness desire appreciation. They need to be noticed and acknowledged for what they do. They care greatly about how they are regarded by their peers, neighbors, and relatives—especially the more wealthy and successful ones. These people are more conventional and are concerned with proper manners, etiquette, and social graces. Acceptance often means "not rocking the boat." Those of the SIXness pathway are often more joiners than loners. They seek status.

Much attention in the energy stream of SIXness is given over to family issues. Many children face themes such as family approval, sibling rivalry, the need for attention and acceptance, and possible enmeshment. A primary need is to learn how to love and relinquish the family at the same time. The theme of the family unit (and social group), which is SIXness, vibrates between FIVEness (personal freedom and newness) and SEVENness (discovering oneself apart, in aloneness and study). One of the most important balances and integrations in life is to learn how to remain close to one's own blood relations and peers while also learning to build one's identity and establish a new "family," where love and caring can be expressed from one's own center and focus. A person who is strong in the energy of SIXness, who has deep family ties, will almost surely have to move away from family to a new location, in order to become his or her own person before returning to the area of family residence. This step is often painful and excrutiatingly difficult, especially when there is much closeness among mother, father, siblings and family members. The greatest "support" of a clan for one of its members is to empower that single individual to move out and establish a new, independent identity.

Nurturing does not mean stifling. Because certain people need to feel accepted, it is sometimes possible to hold them emotionally needy and dependent by keeping them contained in a "nest" of judgments, personal preferences, opinions, intimidation, censure and other manipulative devices. It is also wisdom to love someone without being too protective, thereby shielding that individual from his or her life's lessons and experience—not allowing others to make mistakes and not loving and standing by them throughout the necessary learning process.

The energy of SIXness is extremely valuable to our society. In it there is great caring and kindness. There is the generosity of the heart and the purse. Friendship and devotion are especially commendable when there are no strings attached—when sincere affection becomes its own reward. Genuine SIXness appreciates others for themselves, not because they conform or agree with particular viewpoints or styles. There is no more beautiful experience than to work together in a group toward a noble, common cause that may benefit society or mankind. In the genuine spirit of group cooperation, the power of networking increases, equaling the square of the number of individual participants. In the absence of competition, comparison, and jealousy, SIXness enhances the good of the community, the cohesive welfare of the family unit, and the future health of cities and nations. As such, it expresses a dynamic healing potency within society.

Strengths from the Energy of SIXness

These are the primary gifts of the stream of SIXness: an enjoyment of conviviality and group togetherness; an ability to use personal, artistic creativity for the entertainment of family and society; extending procreation into the creative rearing and caring for the child; a love of the home, mate, children, relatives, pets, and the needy; a sense of fair play and the comforts of friendship, which encourage sharing at ease; an invitation to individuals to participate in a larger collective gathering; the ideal of service to the group becomes a dynamic incentive for sublimating personal energy drives and using resources for larger areas of need.

Values and Creativity of SIXness

Outstanding values and creative aspects of the energy of SIXness include the following:

1) Gratitude — being thankful and able to express warmth and friendly feelings toward our benefactors.

2) Generosity — the ability to give more than the minimum requirement; being willing to extend ourselves.

3) Caring — the capacity to feel for others and stand by them, especially in times of need, even when it is inconvenient.

4) Thoughtfulness — the ability to show empathy and consideration for others.

One of the great areas of creativity for people expressing the energy of SIXness is the marvelous capacity for cultivating friendships. These people are able to enjoy good conversation, and they can stimulate discussion and explore a theme together. They often build better bonding through parlor games, lectures, panels, debates, neighborhood barbecues, cook-outs, parties, reunions, fund drives, outings, anniversary celebrations, birthday remembrances, and outdoor concerts in the park. They observe customs and holidays and enjoy intercultural sharings of special artistic and spiritual significance. They find their best outlets in participating in civic events in the community; they work toward enriching the environment; they support local charities, and they feel, think and act with social concern. In a conversation, a friend of mine, now deceased, has described SIXness musically:

> The SIXTH tone of the C-major scale is 'A'—the note by which all the instruments of the orchestra are brought into accord. The pitch is given by the plaintive oboe, comparable to the lamb, among lions before the Lord.

Observing the Spectrum of SIXness Energy

The pathway of SIXness emphasizes friends, family, group, and home, which extends into the community. Actually, this energy flows through the child in all the developmental stages. The infant's first sight often views mother, father, siblings, pets, and the walls, furniture, rooms, carpets, sofas, etc., and many auditory and kinesthetic impressions arise within the home. Friends become important early on, and if a child has an early predisposition for needs that focus on the energy of SIXness, then a warm and friendly environment, filled with nurturing family members, peers, pets, and other friendly additions is essential. Positive experiences in the energy of SIXness insure the modeling for good manners, culture, friendly conversation, kindness to one another, and a caring concern for the well-being of others.

If SIXness is not present early—if the home is unfriendly, and/or caretakers are threatening or stifling, it is often more difficult for family members to relate with each other and the outside world. Many antisocial and sociopathic behaviors begin with the absence of early nurturing and mutual respect and kindness for one another inside the walls of the home.

Too much family togetherness causes enmeshment and an imprisonment within the family structure. Excessive SIXness often means a fusion of individuals' boundaries, so that personhood is denied in the name of loyalty to the group. Often, status-seeking and hidden family secrets cause individuals within the biological clan to remain crippled and non-functioning in the outside world. They may grow up with a sense of shame that prohibits self-discovery and awareness of their deeper identity in the eternal.

The Underdeveloped Expression of SIXness (–6)

"Living in the fast lane," the person resents responsibilities and social obligations.

It is undesirable and uncomfortable to join a group.

"Maverick" behaviors lack social graces, manners or etiquette.

The person is not nurturing and is not a good provider for others.

Renegade, slob-like attitudes come across as uncouth.

The house is not a home; just a "roof over one's head" and a place to "bed down" for a night.

There is no remorse, regret, or caring.

The person has difficulty sharing with others.

Negative role models are preferable.

Often, a person must learn to give to others what he/she has not received.

Poor timing results in putting one's foot in one's mouth.

There is little desire to contribute to the social welfare.

Sociopathic behaviors damage the good of others and society.

Antisocial attitudes dislike others' company.

It is difficult to sustain a warm, loving and sharing relationship.

Regular job hours are a distasteful infringement on personal freedom.
The person will do work that is illegal or harmful to others—just to "make a living."
Who cares how my behavior may affect others?
I do only what I feel like doing.
"The world owes me a living."
Erratic behavior makes the person untrustworthy.
The ethical dimension of life is largely unawakened.
The person is not a good mixer.

The Balanced Expression of SIXness (6)

The person gains friends by being a friend to others.
A basic kindness and caring are clearly intended and expressed.
Thoughtfulness for others bestows trust.
Fellowship and companionship are important ingredients of a life.
Gratitude is frequently expressed.
Pleasure and happiness come from nurturing others.
The person lives on friendly terms with family relations.
Appreciation of life and people brings enjoyment.
The family tree may be carefully researched.
Traditions and customs are valued.
Good manners and good taste seek moderation and are pleasing to others.
The person has an active social calendar.
Friendships may include many generations of people.
The person is active in social causes and community projects.
It is a pleasure to visit and spend time chatting.
The home is friendly and filled with entertainment.
Parties and gatherings allow for group interaction and conversation.
"Welcome to the team."

A good citizen is a valuable asset to the community and nation.

The person enjoys loving and being loved.

A basic respect for conventionality is more comfortable with similarities than with differences.

Conformity is often preferable.

Human dignity is to be admired.

The family and group energy wield influence.

The Excessive Expression of SIXness (+6)

Pretentious, status-seeking attitudes "put on the dog."

Glamor and too many creature comforts indicate superficiality and feelings of insecurity.

Narcissistic people must always be the center of attention.

These people always want praise and "fish" for compliments.

Chatter and gossip abound.

Nosy questions are common; these people must be "in the know."

They see too much of others; familiarity breeds contempt.

Life is an act; pretense and pleasing others prevent them from living their own life.

There is too much parenting; too much "smother love."

Everybody is enmeshed and caught up in family issues.

There is more curiosity than caring.

They cannot be alone.

There must be endless strokes.

If not included, they become resentful and feel "left out."

Toadying, placating, and telling others just what they want to hear make them become chameleons.

Social snobbery, "all show," and feelings of superiority give them a false sense of being favored.

Do-gooders become resented.

"I must be entertained."

These people feed off others' "news" and live vicariously
through them.
To be accepted, these people become "two-faced" and
deceitful.
Having replaces being.
They always need to be noticed.

Case Study in the Energies of SIXness

I know a most remarkable woman who personifies the
energy of SIXness. Mrs. D. married early and had children. She was a most caring mother, who also reached out
to needy people in the neighborhood. She cared for stray
animals who wandered into her home. When her family
left home, Mrs. D. lost no time in getting into community
health care. She saw an obvious need to reach out to
migrant workers and other underprivileged people. She
began modestly, opening a small clinic which served med-
ical needs of those too poor to be taken in by other profes-
sionals. Through grants and the efforts of a small, loyal
staff, Mrs. D. expanded her services until she found herself coordinator and director of seven health care centers.
She was able to open a prenatal care unit, as well as den-
tal, home health and counseling facilities. Knowing her as
a true friend and working with her through the counseling
department, I saw the many long hours of caring Mrs. D.
put in for people who may well have died had they not
found help through these facilities. Mrs. D. was proud of
her grandchildren as well, and could often be seen interacting with some of the staff as though they were family.
Even when finally weakened from overextending herself,
Mrs. D. kept current with new programs to help the poor.
I have not seen her since her "retirement" from her organization, but I am sure she will find new horizons of caring
in the years ahead. It will always remain one of my fon-

dest memories and privileges to have worked with Mr. D. and shared her friendship.

Expanding the Energy of SIXness

1) Plan a family outing: go on a picnic, a boating trip, hike, etc.

2) Join one community organization: conservationists, Sierra Club, Women's Guild, Elks, Rotary, Lions, Boy Scouts, Little League, 4-H, etc.

3) Become involved in one social or community cause.

4) Visit a nursing home and spend one hour a week making the residents feel loved and appreciated.

5) Give three compliments a day (sincere ones) to others.

6) Call your mother and/or father and say you love them.

7) Write somebody from your past and wish them well.

8) Offer to bring a dish for the next potluck dinner.

9) Invite some friends over for dinner. Prepare the dinner for them.

10) Bless people that have been a thorn in your side or who may still be difficult for you. Notice how they are your "teacher" and what issues or sides of yourself they mirror back to you.

11) Review your day: can you think of three ways that you were thoughtful toward someone else today?

12) Which teacher taught you the most? Why? How?

13) In your present relationship how much are you giving to enrich each day? Are there ways you could give more? Where? How?

14) Try to feel where your children are heading. Can you distinguish between what they may want vs. what *you* want for them? Are you attuned closely to how they feel?

15) What have you done today and recently that has added constructively to society?

The Energy of SEVENness

When a person is in relation with silence, he is not burdened by his knowledge. The eye that comes from the broad surface of silence sees the whole, and not merely the parts, because it sees with the broad, all-embracing gaze of silence itself. The word that comes out of silence embraces the object with the original power that it receives from silence, and the object adds something of this power to its own substance.

— Max Picard

Keys to SEVENness

The energies of SEVENness center in one's connectedness with God–deeper knowledge and solitude. To discover how linked you may be with the stream of SEVENness, consider the following questions:

1) Do you have a strong sense of why you are in this lifetime and what you are here to do?

2) Is God foremost in your consciousness throughout the day?

3) Do you enjoy being alone for a part of each day?

4) Do you find regular times for meditation and prayer?

5) Do you feel you know yourself–apart from your work?

6) Do you try to live by a definite sense of values?

7) Do you believe there is a plan and a purpose to each person's life?

8) Is it important for you to gain deeper knowledge and understanding?

9) Is it clear to you how what you give out to others comes back to you?

10) Do you often feel another world or dimension filling you and the world that you live in here on earth?

The more questions you have answered *yes* to, the stronger your connection with the stream of SEVENness is likely to be.

The Energy of SEVENness in World Symbolism

SEVENness means universal Law, with which all things are held in balance. The energy of SEVENness brings spiritual realization and illumination. In this sense SEVENness is more active in its quietness, waiting for the moment behind the outer turmoil, when the time is right to bring through a higher world of possibilities. With SEVENness there is a "holy emanation of power that descends from on high."[1]

In the stream of SEVENness, persons make contact with various spiritual teachings, religions and higher psychology. Inspiration (THREE) couples with purposeful activity (FOUR) to bring in the new order of consciousness and understanding. In the Pythagorean school of Crotona, the triangle (THREE) and the square (FOUR) were felt to lead to fruitful meditations. Insights into the three-dimensional world—mineral, vegetable, and animal kingdoms—lead into the heights of the fourth dimension and the balanced androgynous human being: the man with a balanced male-female polarity will relate with the woman who expresses the harmony of her own female-male polarity of energies. Thus, the mystic marriage and friendship between the sexes will replace the earlier consciousness of desire and the urge to procreate.

SEVEN was held to be a sacred number by the Hebrews and also by the Moslems, who even to this day describe seven climates, seven seas, seven heavens and as many hells. Certain Rabbis mention that the body of Adam was made of seven handfuls of mould, taken from seven stages of the earth.[2]

1C. Heline, p. 56.
2G. Oliver, p. 169.

The Theosophic philosophy counted SEVEN proper-
ties in the human being: the divine golden human; the
inward holy body from fire and light, like pure silver; the
elemental human; the mercurial growing paradisiacal
human; the martial soul-like human; the venerine—
according to outward desire; and the solar human—an
inspector of the wonders of God. This philosophy also
mentioned SEVEN powers of nature: binding, attraction,
anguish, fire, light, sound and body.[3]

There are many well-known groups of SEVEN in
world symbology: SEVEN notes of the musical scale,
SEVEN colors of the rainbow and spectrum, SEVEN
vowel sounds of speech, SEVEN wonders of the ancient
world, SEVEN days of the week, SEVEN days of creation
(Genesis), the SEVEN seas, and the SEVEN layers of
skin.

We read of SEVEN virtues: strength, faith, prudence,
temperance, justice, charity, and hope; we also hear of
SEVEN vices: wrath, pride, idleness, gluttony, envy, luxury and avarice; in Theosophical literature and other spiritual writings, we read of SEVEN root races, moving mankind toward illumination and initiation. Every person has
SEVEN senses: seeing, smelling, touching, tasting, hear-
ing, intuition and bi-location.

Guy Murchie, in his writings in science and philosophy, mentions SEVEN mysteries of life: the abstract
nature of the universe, the interrelatedness of all creatures, omnipresence of life, the polarity principle, transcendence, germination of worlds and divinity.[4]

In Buddhism we read of SEVEN gods: Hotei, with the
potbelly and serene soul, god of contentment and good
nature; Jurojin, god of longevity and wisdom; Fukuro-

[3]G. Oliver, p. 179.
[4]G. Murchie, *The Seven Mysteries of Life* (Boston: Houghton Mifflin, 1978),
p. 647–659.

kuju, god of long life; Daikoku, patron god of farmers and
good humor; Bishamon, carrying a spear and a pagoda,
god of wealth, a warrior who is also a missionary; Ebisu,
god of honest labor; and Benten, goddess of the sea,
accomplished in the arts and playing the biwa, a
mandolin-like instrument.[5]

The Expression of SEVENness
in the Human Temperament

The energies of the SEVEN pathway awaken intuitive
thinking. SIXness looks outward, more to the company of
others and group activities; SEVENness moves inward to
the interior, observing mind and to the soul that watches
in silence. Our deeper self seeks meaning in life and the
essential significance of events and relationships. Those
who are strongly connected to the energies of SEVENness
usually investigate the mysteries of life: they are never
satisfied with formulas or superficial, slick labels or quick
explanations. In touch with their vertical mind and soul
depth, they will find the hidden doors opening into larger
dimensions of truth, understanding, and cosmic life.
Questions most likely to be asked by those who are
attuned to the path of SEVENness include the following:

1) Who am I?
2) Why was I created?
3) Why have I come into this lifetime?
4) What is my true path and purpose?
5) What makes persons the way they are?
6) Who made me; what is the Creator like?
7) What comes after this lifetime? What happens
   to me?

---

[5]C. Whittaker, *An Introduction to Oriental Mythology* (Secaucus, NJ:
Chartwell, 1989), p. 116.

The greatest aspiration of SEVENness is to feel an interior connection with the Eternal; each individual makes his or her own contact, and it is this interior linking that is the only real source of strength in life.

In this time of history, we can clearly observe peoples' growing desire to experience directly the Presence of a Higher Power. The rapid rise of twelve-step programs and other support groups are fast becoming the new churches of the future. In my own experience with such groups, a fascinating process unfolds: from the building of mutual trust and from intense sharing among the group members, slowly each individual begins to look inward, asking the eventual questions, "After all that has happened to me so far, being able now to express my feelings accurately, what will I do with the rest of my life? What am I really here to do and to be?" Sooner or later, the group process points each participant back into the interior relationship between man and woman and the Creator of all life.

In the process of integrating SIXness and its group activity with the inner, solitary life of SEVENness, a new inner dialogue begins to occur. The process of examining our life begins to flower in us, especially as we ask and reflect on the now accepted twelve-step approach, which I adapted from the AA program:

1) I am aware that certain parts of my life now need to be taken in hand.

2) I am receptive to a Higher Power, greater than myself, that works with me in this process.

3) I now open myself, as completely as possible, to be receptive to the leading of the Higher Power.

4) I release all denial and fear, in order to take an honest inventory of my life in all departments: physical, emotional, mental, and intuitive-spiritual.

5) I admit to the Higher Power, to myself and to another trusted human being the exact nature of my errors and ignorance.

6) I am ready now to respond to the Higher Power and to take the necessary steps to correct my defects in behavior and character. ˙

7) I humbly ask for help in my willingness to work on my shortcomings.

8) I make a list of all people I may have harmed, and as much as I can, I move to make amends to all.

9) I make amends to such persons, wherever possible, except where it might injure them or others.

10) I will continue to keep up my personal inventory, and when I am wrong, I will admit it.

11) Through reflection, meditation and prayer, I daily will seek to deepen my conscious contact with the Higher Power. I pray for greater insight and understanding of God's Will for me, and I pray for the empowerment to live the life I am here to live.

12) Where possible, I will try to share this program and process with all others who are in need.

In this type of program, there is a deep longing for spirituality and a connection with the Divine. Such an approach may or may not be religious—that is, tied into particular organized religions, theologies, or belief systems. One's spirituality is more than just adhering outwardly to a religion: it is one's personal relationship with the Holy. From genuine spirituality, organic changes begin to occur in one's life; they usually last longer, since they are changes that are truly desired, not imposed by some outer authority. In the energy of SEVENness, therefore, it is important for each individual to feel and know spiritual attunement. Each of us works out our wholeness; the Great Longing calls each person forward toward greater expression and completion.

Attitudes and Behaviors of SEVENness

From the perspective of SEVENness, every individual comes into a lifetime to express a unique purpose, in ways that nobody else can imitate or duplicate. There is meaning and significance to everything that we experience. What ultimately matters is to be true and faithful to the path we have chosen. A deeper Plan is at work throughout our life; we are helped by those visible and invisible. Nothing happens by chance.

People who are strong in the energy of SEVENness may prefer to work alone, in quiet places. They do not need people to the degree that others may, and they need more privacy and solitude for their lives to unfold and to sustain attunement with the deeper forces of life. They do not usually seek publicity; often, their direction is more mystical: they seem to be motivated and inspired from more invisible spiritual resources that cannot be externally measured or defined. Such resonance strengthens their communion with life.

SEVEN people tend to be more private and highly selective. They don't talk a lot, but they are always observant, watching carefully others' movements and listening to their comments. They find deeper friendship in spiritual affinity, which knows no boundaries and cuts across ages, cultures, creeds and nationalities. The real attraction is through consciousness. As the writer, Richard Bach, points out:

> The bond that links your true family is not one of blood, but of respect and joy in each other's life.

> Rarely do members of one family grow up under
> the same roof.[6]

The greatest rapport, therefore, emerges between two
people who are traveling in the same direction—toward
the unknown. Such travelers see through whatever is
shallow, false, or distorted. There is an inner bedrock of
faith—a certainty in the face of the unseen—that a Higher
Power is directing and inspiring human lives.

People of the SEVEN path often enjoy their own kinds
of quiet reflection, meditation, prayerful thought and
silent, reverent contemplation.

Those of the energy of SEVENness are lifelong students who seek deeper knowledge. Careful reading and
study quicken the intuition and insight. It is helpful to
specialize in some field of learning, and those on the path
of SEVENness may return to school for deeper study, or
may develop their own program of investigation and
research.

Sometimes one room or a certain area of the home will
be set aside as a shrine for remembrance that magnetizes
the Light and focuses the power of the infinite Presence.
Watchwords are sometimes used to center the consciousness. They may come from the Bible, Daily Word, Daily
Bread, the Hazelton series of daily meditations, or from
anywhere. They may resemble the following keynotes:

> I rest in God as the earth rests in space.[7]

> Be not afraid, neither be dismayed: for the Lord thy
> God is with you wherever you go. (*Joshua 1:9*).

6R. Bach, *Illusions* (New York: Dell Pub., 1977), p. 84.

7M. Rasmussen, quoted by F. A. Newhouse, "Meditation," taped lecture
(Escondido, CA: Christward Ministry, January 5, 1955).

Persons attuned to the energy of SEVENness often affirm the words, "Come ye apart a while." Aloneness need not be lonely. Walks in nature, climbing high mountain trails, wandering private paths in the woods, viewing fields and flowers and the mighty Redwoods or a great waterfall can invite visits of Angels, unseen helpers of God, or perhaps a person may hear sudden music of great bells and celestial choruses, ringing through the Silence. Ceremonies and rituals, observed reverently, can bring openings into invisible worlds of light and beauty that surround us.

Strengths from the Energy of SEVENness

In their quiet ways, people who are strong in the energy of SEVENness express many sterling strengths. They often live more unnoticed in their quiet refinement and serenity. They often are more comfortable in the worlds of the invisible; less so in the mundane and concrete world. Their life style is one of simplicity, and they prefer to avoid the complications and bustle of life. Through inner attunement with deeper wellsprings of strength, they learn how to withstand outer uncertainties. They can be content with who they are, while yet looking toward the greater unknown. They respond intuitively, finding solutions that may be unexpected and unplanned, seemingly arising out of nowhere. These people express a love of purity and truth, able to surrender themselves into a power that is greater than they are, yet feeds them. They have a penetrating insight, and they investigate thoroughly before making conclusions. It is not unusual to find in these people a profound sense of humor that shows an awareness of life's perspectives. They may be highly unorthodox and spiritually original. They can work better "with" groups, not in them. Only a few people get to know them or get close to them. Individuals who are strong in the energy of SEVENness learn from the great teachers of life. They listen in the silence, sensing the great chain of beings who fill the ladder of Light throughout the dimensions of cosmic life. They are keen observers.

Values and Creativity of SEVENness

These are the outstanding values and areas of creativity for the path of SEVENness:

1) Faith—the ability to live with conviction and trust that does not question the ways of a larger energy flow—the direction of Divine Order.
2) Reverence—profound respect, mingling with love and awe for all creation.
3) Truth—clear perception of what is.
4) God Awareness—the inner sensing and knowing that all lives are sustained and directed by a larger Power and Presence.
5) Exampleship—living out daily what one believes and affirms.
6) Innocence—to be washed pure by not repeating errors.
7) Simplicity—freedom from pose, artificiality, or affectation.
8) Serenity—poise in the midst of testings and difficult circumstances.

In creativity and work areas, those of the SEVEN stream usually go into more highly specialized areas, such as scientific research, psychology, or metaphysics. By nature they are investigative and are interested in the more hidden, esoteric sides of life. They aim for perfection in what interests them, and they look for depth in their relationships. Their intuition and thinking lead them to feeling and action. They often have a design for their living, such as these life rules of Mahatma Gandhi:

> I will be truthful.
> I will suffer no injustice.
> I will be free from fear.
> I will not use force.
> I will be of good will to all persons.[8]

Observing the Spectrum of SEVENness Energy

The pathway of SEVENness releases energies that focus on self-knowledge, solitude, the inner dialogue with one's deeper self, and the mystical quest for Truth and contact with the ever present, all-encompassing Divinity. SEVENness usually takes us into the investigative fields of science, psychology, metaphysics, and esoteric studies. More often, these areas of our life become increasingly important from our late thirties onward. For some people, SEVENness emerges in their life when the pleasures and pursuits of the world are frustrated or exhausted; meaning becomes more important than just doing.

It is possible to live one's entire life "on the rim," stimulated and tossed about by the demands of others and the distractions and limited pleasures of sensation. In the deeper flow of SEVENness energy, people tend to draw back; they move more into stillness and inner reflection, and they evaluate their interests, pursuits, and motivations. When this energy is not sufficiently present, people demonstrate less centeredness and inner attunement; they simply react to outer bombardments and crises. Their life then becomes more of an adherence to others' wishes

---

[8]Mahatma Gandhi, quoted in F. A. Newhouse, *Quest Lessons*, vol I, p. 213.

than a response to inner leadings. When SEVENness is extremely recessive in people's lives, there is rarely any sense of cause and effect, or awareness of how one's choices today will shape the life experiences of the future. Too much SEVENness results in elitist attitudes and feelings of superiority. Life becomes an exclusive contest between "them and us," often resulting in unhealthy seclusion and isolation from the world.

The Underdeveloped Expression of SEVENness (-7)

Too much time spent with others keeps one ignorant about oneself.

The person does not live out of his or her own center.

There is no philosophy of life—no sense of meaning.

The person does not feel comfortable about looking within.

Inner reflection is avoided.

Often, a Superior Power is denied.

The person does not like to be alone.

There is little sensing of one's Path in life.

Attunement to higher sources of empowerment is rare.

Abstract thinking is difficult.

There is not much interest in the great Teachings of the Ages.

The spiritual heritage of mankind is deemed unimportant.

The person lacks his or her own essence and looks to others for a sense of identity.

The person lacks the necessary knowledge and depth.

Character is suspect.

Silence awakens alarm and fear.

The Balanced Expression of SEVENness (7)

Silence is golden.

Seek meaning in events and experiences.

Gather wisdom and knowledge.
The truth sets one free.
Holy expectancy makes life a continuous adventure.
Faith brings the unseen into visibility.
Simplicity, purity, and depth are necessary virtues.
The person prefers privacy and solitude.
Quiet observation yields large rewards.
The person is reserved, quietly listening in the silence.
Meditative, prayerful times and contemplation are deeply
    valued.
There is a tendency toward perfectionism and accuracy.
The person may be oriented toward metaphysics and eso-
    teric studies.
Seek to penetrate life's mysteries.
Keep life consecrated.
Shun small talk, except when necessary.
Objectivity sometimes may seem dispassionate.
Life is best when lived "beside still waters" of the soul.
A life lived with interior focus does not seek outer renown
    or glory.
Be highly selective.
Try to keep conditions ideal.
Life is best when lived from a vertical perspective.
Reverence for all life is a necessity.
Life is a journey, leading to illumination.
There are dimensions to life that are mystical and filled
    with awe.
Self-realization is paramount.
Be discerning!

The Excessive Expression of SEVENness (+7)

Locked up in silence, the person becomes unreachable
    and unreal.
The person may become too elitist, too austere and too
    "precious."

The ivory tower of the intellect proves to be too abstract;
the person becomes an "egghead."
A superior attitude makes one aloof.
The person likes to play "the guru."
Overly pious and somber behavior is pretentious and
phony.
"I deserve to be waited on because I am special."
Life becomes too reclusive and the person tries to avoid
the world.
There is a disdain for the lowly.
Too much asceticism pervades one's life.
Intolerance makes others feel less worthy.
A "Holier than Thou" attitude fills the air.
A fanatical streak proclaims, "My way is the only way."
"You come to me."
Sanctimonious smugness inflates the ego.
The person exaggerates his or her calling.
The saintly pose feigns holiness.
Spiritual pride and "feeling favored" make one
condescending.
The person becomes too restrictive.
"Playing God" seems natural.
Annoyance surfaces when the person must extend himself
or herself beyond the parameters of his or her own
choosing.
The person will never put himself or herself out for
another's need.

Case Study in the Energy of SEVENness

The most remarkable woman I have known this lifetime
demonstrates the very highest qualities of SEVENness.
Reverend Newhouse is a spiritual teacher and the author
of many books on spiritual subjects. Through the years
she has spoken to many Theosophical and other groups.
Her orientation is Christian mysticism, and she and her

husband founded a nondenominational retreat center in 1940, in Escondido, California. For more than sixty-five years, she has been a spiritual teacher and an inspiration to many. She is quiet and observant, always radiating joy and a loving, yet unsentimental, way. Her primary teaching area is the kingdom of the Angels, and she has written and spoken many times on this unique topic. For me, it is Reverend Newhouse's special gift to be able to talk about Christ and make him real in our world today as a living presence and inspiration to humanity. SEVENness emanates from this woman: she is a lover of nature and its mysteries, and she has been a friend to many animals that she has adopted as strays through the years. She is able to see deeply into the meaning of lives and events, offering insights, but encouraging each individual to work through to necessary solutions. She is a world traveler, who sees very deeply into countries and places, especially those great energy points on the planet that empower all lives. I remember her simple statement to me once as I prepared to walk in the mountains: "Remember: *love* everything!" It has been a rare privilege to serve with Reverend Newhouse in her work for more than twelve years, and I shall always be grateful for her friendship. Her deep understanding of spiritual and esoteric teachings has been the gift she has given to thousands of persons for many years.

Expanding the Energy of SEVENness

1) Agree to spend just 20 minutes a day, by yourself alone, in quiet reflection. Consider one of the following themes daily:

- The Light that fills me;
- The meaning of my life – what am I here for?
- The ideals I most value;

- What this day is teaching me;
- The Christ of this planet;
- God shining through me;
- What I came to do this lifetime;
- My most important overcoming this incarnation;
- My most crucial immediate goal.

2) Begin to realize how much your thoughts and attitudes draw to you the conditions of your life.

3) Develop a "values inventory," in which you include the three most important ingredients in your life.

4) What would you say to a person who asks you, "Who is God?"

5) How would you answer a child who asks you, "Where is God?"

6) Mention an incident in your life when unexpected good happened to you.

7) In what areas of your life would you refuse to compromise?

8) Read for 15 minutes a day from the various spiritual treasuries of mankind:

- The Vedas
- Sermons of the Buddha
- Analects of Confucius
- *Tao Te Ching* of Lao Tzu
- The 4 Gospels—Matthew, Mark, Luke, John (New Testament)
- The Parables of Christ
- *The Prophet*, by Kahlil Gibran
- The Psalms
- The Koran
- The Baha'i teachings

- Poetry of Rumi
- *Disciplines of the Holy Quest—*
  Flower A. Newhouse
- Essays of Emerson
- *Hymn of the Universe,* by Teilhard de Chardin
- *A Candle of Vision,* AE (George Russell)
- *Reflections on the Christ,* David Spangler
- *Letters of the Scattered Brotherhood,*
  (Ed. Mary Strong)
- *Christ in You,* (Anonymous)
- *Daily Word,* Unity
- *The Science of Mind,* Ernest Holmes
- Hazleton Series of Daily Meditations

The Energy of EIGHTness

Let every soul be subject unto the higher powers. For there is no power but of God: the powers that be are ordained of God. . . . Whosoever resists the power resists the ordinance of God . . . : for he is the minister of God to thee for good.

Be not overcome with evil, but overcome evil with good.

—Romans 13:1,2,4; 12:21

Put up again thy sword into its sheath.

—John 18:11

Eight[ness] is a symbol of the intimate union which subsists between two minds which are knit and joined together by these two genial affections.

—George Oliver

Keys to EIGHTness

Themes of EIGHTness center in areas of power, authority, control and success. To see how deeply you may be linked with this power stream, consider these questions:

1) Does it bother you when you are not in control of situations or relationships?

2) Is it important for you to set limits with others?

3) In most matters are you the one who makes the final decision?

4) Is winning and being successful important for you?

5) Are money and finances an important part of your life?

6) Are there quite a few areas of your life where you wield authority?

7) Do you manage people well?

8) Is it difficult for you to admit to someone you are wrong?

9) Is it important for you to have lots of money?

10) Will you fight for justice whenever necessary?

The more questions you have answered *yes*, the more strongly connected you are likely to be to the stream of EIGHTness.

The Energy of EIGHTness in World Symbolism

In its higher forms of expression, EIGHTness expresses energies that are powerful and cosmic. It has been called the number of resurrection[1] and signifies good judgment and regeneration. EIGHTness means obedience to the heavenly vision; those strongly connected to EIGHTness have a good sense of what is right. They are able to discern the good, and therefore cannot claim ignorance if they make a decision that is unworthy of the Highest.

EIGHT Beatitudes lead to triumph in the teachings of the Christ as presented in the Gospel of Matthew, chapter 5:

1) Openness and receptivity to the Spirit;
2) Capacity to mourn;
3) Meekness (teachableness);
4) Desire for righteousness;
5) Mercy;
6) Purity of heart;
7) Ability to be a peacemaker;
8) Suffering for the sake of righteousness.

The esoteric number of the Christ is 888, and the symbol for the resurrection of life.

According to the Egyptians, EIGHT is the symbol for the serpent with the tail in its mouth. For the Jews, a baby is circumcised on his EIGHTH day of life. EIGHTness, on its side, becomes infinity. The Pythagoreans identified in man EIGHT organs of knowledge: "sense, phantasy, art, opinion, prudence, science, wisdom and mind."[2]

From a spiritual and psychological point of view, EIGHTness refers to the "Dweller on the threshold," the monster armed with the sword of truth—the tester that cuts through the middle of EIGHTness, forcing each of us to decide between our higher and lower self. The "minister to thee for good," as it is called by St. Paul (Romans

---

[1]C. Heline, p. 65.
[2]G. Oliver, p. 193.

13:4), or the "Dweller," named by the psychologist, Carl
Jung, forces each of us to release the lesser for the greater
in the midst of temptations, power struggles, ambition,
jealousy and pride, especially revolving around issues that
concern money. EIGHTness administers the scales of justice. Like an hourglass, EIGHTness connects higher Law
with earthly justice and legal procedures. It is the number
of "the inevitable."[3] The two circles of EIGHT indicate that
we reap what we have sown.

The Expression of EIGHTness
in the Human Temperament

The energies of EIGHTness focus in a person's mind and
in the area of willpower. Lessons of SEVENness—spiritual
awareness, knowing the laws and principles of the universe, and inner centeredness—are now directed outward
toward the management of worldly concerns and business. With the stream of EIGHTness comes a strong desire
to control and administer through power and authority.
People on this path are determined to be successful. Con-
trolled emotions often conceal an enormous ambition and
the will to be right and victorious.

These people want to be in charge; they want to make
the decisions. They set the policies, and others are
expected to follow orders. Permission must first be
granted before someone else is allowed to make changes.
Good judgment and good management emerge from a
definite protocol, which must always be obeyed. In the
most open demonstrations of EIGHTness, there is always
a desire for consensus: the outcome is best achieved
through agreement among the corporate group, not
merely the "heavy fist" of one person at the top of the
pyramid, in the power position. The futurist writer, John

[3]F. H. & H. Curtiss, *Key to the Universe*, p. 285.

Naisbitt, describes this new approach of management by consensus when he says:

> The ethic of participation is spreading bottom up across America and is radically altering the way we think people in institutions should be governed. Citizens, workers, and consumers are demanding and getting a greater voice in government, business and the marketplace.
>
> People, whose lives are affected by a decision must be part of the process of arriving at that decision . . .; participatory democracy has seeped into the core of our value system. Its greatest impact will be in government and corporations.[4]

Thus, we can look at our times today as a challenge for each person to learn to use power benevolently. It is neither the time for aggression and autocracy, nor the time for absenting and giving one's power to someone else. Those in power do best when they use their influence to empower others to achieve noble and worthy outcomes. Delegating some of the responsibility is one way to acquire competent partners and helpers.

When everyone is working together for the greater good and the best outcome, then there is no longer any dominant enforcer; instead, all people share a common vision, and tremendous power is released. For those who prefer progress, not control, suspicion, intimidation, and confrontation are no longer necessary. Suppression and exploitation can be redirected toward greater productivity and creativity for everyone.

---

[4]J. Naisbitt, *Megatrends* (New York: Warner, 1982), p. 159.

Attitudes and Behaviors of EIGHTness

People who are strongly connected to the energy of
EIGHTness must find some creative outlet that allows
them to exercise constructive management and authority.
They cannot suppress the power center in themselves, or
they will become frustrated and passive-aggressive.
Nobody can "hide one's light under a bushel," nor is it
wise to try to "boss" the wrong people in situations that
are inappropriate. Those who naturally enjoy management do well to seek out employment where their leadership and supervisory skills are needed. Otherwise, their
tendency to try and "take over" will alienate them from
friends. If these people enter a power position, they do
well in learning the art of negotiation.

Those who emanate the power of EIGHTness wield a
strong sense of command and control. They tend to want
to keep people and events within the reins of their authority. They do not like emotional display, yet often, by their
very controlling nature, they force others to "break out"
and defy their continuous orders. They tend to want to
keep others within certain boundaries, thus setting up
conditions and feelings of defiance and resentment in
those who also have legitimate needs and desires to be
themselves.

Strengths from the Energy of EIGHTness

The outstanding qualities of EIGHTness are as follows:
there is a strong need to make decisions and enforce them
at all times; at its best, the energy of EIGHTness means
self-command and an inner obedience to the very highest
principles of justice and fairness; there is good judgment
and dependable follow-through; a love of success and
abundance leads to a strong financial position; the energy
of EIGHTness takes charge in all situations.

Values and Creativity of EIGHTness

Outstanding values of the energy of EIGHTness include the following:

1) Justice—living one's life in accord with the laws— social and universal.
2) Good Judgment—the ability to assess life situations with fairness and keen discernment.
3) Stewardship—being responsible for one's property and material possessions; using well whatever one has earned or been given charge of.
4) Righteousness—living by what is right.
5) Self-discipline—demonstrating self-control and appropriate behavior.

Creatively, those who are expressing the energy of EIGHTness tend to become active in business and finance. Administration, supervision, and the world of corporate structures are often areas of interest. These people want to be successful, and they respect top performance. Investments, of either time and money, are measured for their profitable returns. What counts is the ability to be decisive and accountable, realizing fully the consequences of their actions. In work situations, people of EIGHTness look to climb the corporate ladder of success, and they generally seek positions of leadership, such as executive, school principal, escrow officer, head contractor, head coach, judge, chief pilot, bank president, labor leader, head of examining board, manager, attorney, etc.

More esoterically, EIGHTness involves dealing with the enemy or adversary within oneself; events arise that make one choose between the higher or lower nature; energy, coiled like a serpent into the figure 8, can be channeled constructively or destructively. A decision determines our real value system and whether we live it or not.

The ancient teacher, Zoroaster, points out the power of this inward confrontation:

> Struggle prayerfully, day and night, with your own fiend, and all life long not to depart from steadfastness, nor allow your proper duty to go out of your hands.[5]

Observing the Spectrum of EIGHTness Energy

EIGHTness is an energy that has to do with power, authority, boundaries, and success. Early in childhood it is helpful for people to learn to express power in ways that empower others. Early expressions of defiance and the courage to say what we are feeling with conviction release the power of the will. Constructive use of the will connects us with a deep part of ourself, called in esoteric teachings the Adonaic self. In this way EIGHTness opens up the power center in people.

If we do not contact the power center within us, we may fail to follow through in areas of our life; we stop short of successful attainment, often losing our boundaries and giving our power away. Or we might become passive-aggressive, trying to express our desires for control and command in ways that are sneaky and deceptive.

When EIGHTness becomes too dominant an energy, we can observe behaviors such as a mania for power and position, tendencies toward cruelty and sadism, and an insatiable hunger for wealth and riches.

---

[5]*The Bible of the World*, ed. R. O. Ballou (New York: Viking Press, 1939), p. 618.

The Underdeveloped Expression of EIGHTness (–8)

Not wanting to become involved, the person remains indecisive.

No boundaries are enforced; the person seems wishy-washy.

There is a need to take charge of situations.

A poverty consciousness comes from too much "other worldliness."

The person does not want to handle money.

A fear of authority and power persists. One's own power is unowned.

There is a fear of failure.

The person allows others to dominate too much.

Financial obligations increase.

There is a lack of policy in one's life.

Passive-aggressive tendencies produce power struggles.

"Pass the buck" and let others make the decisions.

Expect others to enforce the rules.

Ask others to repeat directions again and again.

Allow others to decide, then attack them for making the "wrong" choice.

No limits are set; one's space is frequently invaded.

The Balanced Expression of EIGHTness (8)

Adequate supply, abundance and prosperity fill the universe.

There is a need to assume managerial positions and make decisions.

The person wants to direct and supervise.

Power and control are essential ingredients of life.

The desire for justice is fulfilled through negotiation and legal procedures.

Strong willpower sees the situation through to completion.

Obedience is required and enforced.
Resistance is immediately confronted.
Areas of business and commerce are appealing.
Good stewardship treats property and possessions well.
Money is often wisely invested.
Good judgment prevents mishaps and messes.
The corporate structure amasses power and authority.
Plan and execute!
The person likes to be "on top."
Orders are issued and compliance is demanded, or conse-
    quences will follow.
Seek positions of influence
Mandates will not often allow for interference or delay.
Accountability must be demonstrated; supremacy must be
    proved.
Know when to draw the line. "The buck stops here."
Be decisive; mean what you say and say what you mean.
Look for profit in all areas of life.
Establish policy and avoid any deviation.
Take power and dominion whenever possible.
The greatest act of power empowers others.
Be a benevolent ruler.
The place of supremacy can become a win-win for
    everyone.
"Money speaks."
Compete with strategy, but keep the transaction
    honorable.

The Excessive Expression of EIGHTness (+8)

The mania for power and wealth makes a person hard and
    inflexible.
Part of the game is to manipulate others and control
    them.
The approach to life is too calculating, ruthless, and
    dictatorial.

Even better than winning is getting even.

The person is vengeful, vindictive, cruel, and unmerciful.

Don't take any prisoners!

Be coercive, "rub it in," and humiliate others.

The person uses position to take advantage, not to empower others.

Jealousy results in a person demeaning others and feeling contempt for them.

Never acknowledge anyone other than yourself.

Hostility develops into a vendetta against another person.

The person always has to be right.

In business unscrupulous behaviors are common.

Sadism, the love of inflicting pain on others, reinforces one's sense of power.

Tyranny often takes the form of sarcasm.

Most efforts receive censure.

In relationships, the person attempts to steamroll and stonewall others.

Riches and wealth are hoarded; the person feels he can never get enough.

The opposition must be annihilated.

Hatreds remain unresolved.

Case Study in the Energy of EIGHTness

Denying the natural flow of one's energy through any of the numerical pathways can cause distortions in behavior and harmful responses to life. In the stream of EIGHTness, two people must grant each other their own individual areas of power, without interfering or invading territory. If each individual has his or her area of power and managerial expression, then there is less likelihood of confrontation or suppression. There is a greater possibility for a meeting of minds.

A colleague once told me about a remarkable case involving the energy of EIGHTness: a father, who was physically large and mentally a dictator in the household, began to beat his adolescent son for being "willful and defiant." The boy, deeply hurt and offended, began to vent his anger by beginning to abuse the family pets and hacking apart the flowers in the back yard. He also became aggressive and domineering with the girls he dated. His mother was afraid of the father and remained passive and unsupportive of the boy. A thirst for power and revenge (+8) seethed inside the boy. Fortunately, his church suggested that he get into counseling. The counselor, who clearly recognized the boy's need to vent anger, convinced him to take some karate classes, and he quickly advanced to the level of black belt. He now teaches martial arts and is old enough that his father wisely stays out of his way. They rarely talk.

This story illustrates the example of two individuals locked into extreme concentrates of EIGHTness energy. Had the confrontation between father and son continued, there would surely have been a fatal outcome. Because EIGHTness focuses so strongly in areas of authority, to contact this energy, each of us must learn how to own our personal power and express it in ways that are benevolent and empowering to others. If our power center is denied or assaulted by aggressive confrontation, tragedy often occurs. First, there is usually defensiveness, perhaps in the form of passive-aggressive behaviors; a person may fight or flee the situation. The worst form of the misuse of the energy of EIGHTness is sadism, a desire to hurt or torture others because we have been hurt. Ultimately, we may even try to conquer life by annihilating it, coming to the point of actually hating life itself.

Another distortion of EIGHTness, in its own coercive way, concerns some people's desire to use knowledge about others for power over them. Erich Fromm, the psychologist, calls this the misuse of the secrets of the soul:

> We cannot help desiring to penetrate into the secret of a [person's] soul, into the innermost nucleus which is 'he' or 'she.' A desperate way to know the secret is that of complete power over another person: the power which makes one do what we want, feel what we want, think what we want; which transforms a person into a thing, our thing, our possession. . . . The desire and ability to force [another] to betray his or her secret . . . [reveals] an essential motivation for the depth and intensity of cruelty and destructiveness. . . . The other path to knowing the secret is love.[6]

Power, the dominant theme of EIGHTness, can be expressed constructively or destructively. We are in transitional times on our planet, when the old, Machiavellian approach of intimidation, manipulation, cunning, duplicity and deception in the name of greed, and the mania to control others vies with new, emerging forms of benevolent power that bring fairness and a larger consensus. The Machiavellian approach is never win-win; it is based upon cruelty, oppression, and the fear of lack and losing authority; it seeks to maintain control by keeping others chained in fear, uncertainty, and confusion. Such an approach discourages all alliances and interpersonal networking. It denies coalitions among others by keeping them ignorant, uninformed, and unclear about aims and goals, policies, and responsibilities. By keeping others unclear about jobs, intentions, and procedures, those in power can control more easily through blame and censure. There is no sense of trust, no willingness to listen to another's input and

---

6E. Fromm, p. 29–30.

point of view, no ability to work together as equals for a common purpose. As such people in power positions become more secure in themselves and less rigid in their limited perspectives, they will become more willing to use power to empower others. In the spirit of benevolent rulership and a more flexible meeting of the minds, all persons will discover new ways to express the balanced energy of EIGHTness.

Expanding the Energy of EIGHTness

1) Set clear boundaries in your life. Mean what you say and say what you mean.

2) Make one financial investment and keep informed on its progress.

3) Whom did you empower today?

4) Look at your ways of disciplining: do they promote learning and good direction, or are they punitive and hurtful?

5) Develop a plan of informing someone else about definite consequences before rushing in to punish when it is too late.

6) Develop your ability to benefit others through your own power.

7) If you play a game, such as Monopoly, do you play to win without becoming hostile if you lose?

8) Begin a budget of monthly expenses and charges. Try to keep within your budget. Learn how to balance your own checkbook.

9) In your managerial position, try to develop policies that are win-win for everyone. Can you win without having anyone else be the loser?

10) Before you make your next decision, take a consensus from those around you. See how others think and consider other people's input.

 The
Energy
of
NINEness

God does not offer himself to our finite beings as
a thing all complete and ready to be embraced.
For us he is eternal discovery and eternal
growth. The more we think we understand him,
the more he reveals himself as otherwise. The
more we think we hold him, the further he
withdraws, drawing us into the depths of
himself. The nearer we approach him through
all the efforts of nature and grace, the more he
increases, in one and the same movement, his
attraction over our powers, and the receptivity
of our powers to that divine attraction.

—Teilhard de Chardin

Keys to NINEness

Themes of NINEness focus on compassion, service, and brotherhood. To see how strongly connected you are to this stream of power, consider the following questions:

1) Do you find it necessary to forgive others who have hurt or angered you?

2) Is your perspective on life large enough to accept people who are different in their values and behaviors from you?

3) When others may suffer, do you often rush in to help them?

4) In the midst of loving and giving to others, is it easy for you to hide your own needs?

5) Do you have contact with many different age groups, cultures, religions, and ethnic backgrounds?

6) Are you especially drawn to those who are forgotten or rejected?

7) Do you often rescue stray animals and people?

8) Do you often feel alone in a crowd?

9) Is it difficult for you to say *no*?

10) No matter how you plan, is much of your life a mystery to you?

The more questions that you answered *yes* to, the more likely your connections with the energies of NINEness are strong.

The Energy of NINEness
in World Symbolism

In the symbolism of NINEness, people meet the energies through which they contact their inner selves and express their latent divinity in the world. Illumination thus becomes initiation as NINEness represents "the major vibratory power" that governs human unfoldment.[1] In Chinese teachings, NINE not only describes the earth's center but is also the number of steps leading to the imperial Chinese throne. NINEness represents the triple crown of expression—physical, mental and spiritual. NINE is inclusive, bringing out a unity in the midst of diversity. It is the supreme tester and, with its inevitability, serves the allness of the Totality ahead of itself. In this manner, the Hebrews call NINEness the symbol of truth. It purifies all other numerations and both mysteriously and receptively stands at the crossroads, mighty like a crescendo that powerlessly gives of itself, awaiting transformation.

NINEness is often unappreciated, even in the midst of the goodness and unconditional love that it emanates. Therefore, in the spirit of NINEness a person must not look for reciprocation; instead NINEness must move ahead, flowing like a great river, moving forward with the currents of Infinite Grace.

NINEness signifies the energies of matter, which may change in its forms and vibrations but can never be destroyed. Whenever NINE is multiplied by any number, it always reproduces itself: 9×6 is $54 = 9$.

Saint Gregory and Denis, the Areopagite in their writings, mention (as do biblical writings) NINE orders of Angels:

---

[1]C. Heline, p. 75.

1. Seraphim
2. Cherubim
3. Thrones
4. Dominions
5. Virtues
6. Powers
7. Principalities
8. Archangels
9. Angels

Furthermore, in the Roman Catholic tradition, a novena consists of NINE days of prayerful devotion for the completion of a spiritual objective.

NINEness signifies the end of a process, which leads to transformation. The birth process takes NINE months, and the baby (soul) emerges into the world of living form. Every newborn must go through the process of remembering his or her soul and who he or she is in God. NINEness, therefore, forms a bridge between beginnings and endings—which leads again to new beginnings, hopefully at a higher point on the spiral of unfoldment.

The Expression of NINEness in the Human Temperament

While the energy of EIGHTness emphasizes themes of authority, management, power, decision-making, and control, NINEness instills the process of unconditional love, forgiveness, compassion, and surrender to a deeper mystery: the inscrutable Presence of God at the center of life. NINEness, as an energy, can provide the most humanly uncertain yet ultimately fulfilling experiences in people's lives. We can see an indication of the energy of NINEness when we may go through a period or a relationship in which we may not feel personally rewarded or acknowledged, yet later we can see clearly that we have made a meaningful contribution to the larger totality of life. The energy of NINEness is more "transpersonal;" that is, it comes through individuals while emphasizing all peoples and the upliftment of humankind. NINEness, therefore, centers in areas of great-heartedness: loving and serving the totality and the greater brotherhood, which is always more than the sum of its parts. As individuals, each of us at different times in our lives overcomes our testings by releasing personal interests into the larger needs of humanity. Our consciousness and sensitivity often increase in the midst of suffering and disappointments; we then reach into the immensity consciousness range, where we can feel the heights and depths of the human condition, seeing the paradoxes and mysteries of our existence, filled with joys and sorrows:

> [Such people] suffer and must suffer, but they need not complain; they have known intoxication unknown to the rest, and, if they have wept tears of sadness, they have also poured tears of ineffable joy. That in itself is a heaven for which one never pays what it is worth.[2]

In many ways the other eight pathways might seem to be more filled with assertiveness. NINEness must often wait alertly and eagerly for doors to open in ways that are basically beyond one's personal efforts and control. Readiness, in the midst of an attitude of surrender, brings more long-lasting results than pushing ahead on one's own. In extreme moments—often at the midnight hour—directives for action and mysterious openings suddenly emerge from unexpected sources. "Waiting upon God," with a willingness to do what is required, brings help from the

---

[2]C. Gounod, *The Gift of Music*, ed., Louise Bachelder (Mt. Vernon, NY: Peter Pauper Press, 1975), p. 61.

unknown—from people who may be total strangers—
strange benefactors from the blessings of Divine Grace.

In the stream of NINEness, gain comes through service. Without becoming a martyr, as a person tries to serve
the good of the totality, breakthroughs occur. A balance
emerges between personal needs and self-giving. Sometimes a crisis may cause personal inconvenience, but later
it may be that from a larger perspective it was all necessary. NINEness thus learns to work amid delays, interferences and detours. Even beyond all human efforts, there
is the "right timing" and inscrutability of the Eternal.

The energy of NINEness also means a continuous
shedding of the old, dry skins of the past, a balancing of
old accounts and the process of tying up loose ends and
karmic holdovers from other times and places. In the
midst of "balancing the ledger," there may be some feelings of inevitability and powerlessness, but in the end the
outcome will prove to be beneficial. There is always a great
fragility to life, and a deep, pervading mystery makes us
realize that ultimately, only God is forever; sooner or later,
everything else "comes to pass." Riding out the storm and
keeping centered in the larger flow of life frees us to fulfill
what is asked for so we can work toward deliverance and
transcendence. David Spangler, the spiritual visionary
and writer, describes attitudes of NINEness in these
words:

> Becoming emotionally overwrought at the sins
> and ills of the world . . . will not help you. These
> are responses of glamor usually born of your
> attempts to avoid your own pain and transform-
> ative energies by focusing on lesser emotions.
> What is needed is precise, appropriate, skillful,
> wise, loving and serene action, thought and
> attunement, filled with power and open to the
> true pain of your time and to the potentials of

healing that pain. That universal spirit, which I call the Christ, pours its limitless spirit upon all peoples, upon the land and upon your world as a whole. . . . Carry that spirit outward into action, thought, and relationship to the best of your abilities. If in so doing you find yourself entering into conflict or confrontation with people, institutions, or forces outside yourself, then do so without conflict in your own heart and mind. Do so without seeing these people as being less than brothers and sisters, but part of your wholeness. Do so without losing your vision of the ultimate harmony of all things. . . . Ultimately, all human beings are allies in the single battle against fear and inertia.[3]

For those people who express strongly the energy of NINEness, it is good to remember that God never gives you more than you can handle and surmount. Deeper sources of energy empower every person who tries to release the lesser for the greater. Look for the best in others, even when it seems to be deeply buried and when it would be easier to see the worst. A golden thread links all lives together in a greater unity that is global and universal. Stand up for your ideals, bring forth your dreams and visualize improvement in all conditions. Work tirelessly for greater well-being in every situation.

Attitudes and Behaviors of NINEness

In the energy stream of NINEness, the dominant theme is forgiveness. It is best to release past hurts and disappointments. Seeing with mercy and larger perspective often makes small what once seemed paramount.

---

[3]D. Spangler, *Conversations with John* (Elgin, Il: Lorian Press, 1980), p. 28.

With the energy of NINEness, the tide is going out. But the river flows on and always returns upon another shore. We will meet again in new settings and locations, always seeking the greater harmony on the path. Each lifetime becomes a glowing dewdrop filling the ocean of infinite life. In the brevity of one earthly incarnation, we are fortunate to achieve any intimate bonding and lasting friendship with others. What is truly earned in love can never be lost in Spirit. We see all the shining faces that shimmer in the night. Often, as we reach out to touch each other, we are gone; we sense the great longing—the unspeakable affinity and the instant union, as we pass in silence—together and alone.

A basic kinship unites all people. Each person's breathing in some way warms the frozen stars; the smallest act of kindness never passes unnoticed. There is the great highway of life—the magnificent commonality—the synthesis of bones, brains and heartbeats, meeting in Light. The masks of others become mirrors opening into hidden passages of ourselves. The creatures of our longings, the dreams and hopes that haunt us, become the transformations of our tomorrows, the dawning of the larger self we are becoming; through veils and darkness we penetrate the fires of Love's creative light, and we are forever shaped anew. By shedding the skins of the old, we live out the Taoist saying, "Wear out; become new."

Strengths from the Energy of NINEness

The energy of NINEness, perhaps the most mysterious of all, reveals its own gifts. People demonstrating a balanced expression of NINEness are usually loners in the midst of crowds. They work more in the mainstream but in ways that can be anonymous. Such people contact a broad spectrum of humanity, and they often become advocates and Samaritans to the underdogs. They attract the "lost," the strays, and the outcasts that nobody else wants to be around. People who release the energy of NINEness bring hope into situations filled with agony and sorrow. They recognize the fragility, winsomeness, and transient nature of life. They may meet many persons just once, in passing, but the memories are strong. They feel the mystical union with the world that is like being everywhere and nowhere at once. Such people feel the synthesis of joy and sorrow: the paradox of the comic and the tragic mixing together. In the energy of NINEness, one word or act can change a whole situation; intense feelings may heal or destroy. It is good to keep negotiations open; try not to close doors. For people in the stream of NINEness energy, the vision must always be stronger than personal likes or dislikes. The intention must be to further brotherhood and global unity. The ultimate dedication is to the one Power and the Glory that is immanent yet transcends earthly life. Often, people who live strongly in the energy of NINEness do good without ever knowing it. Their ability to forgive and release the past brings through the empowering currents of new vitality that keeps them moving forward.

Values and Creativity of NINEness

These are the primary values of the stream of NINEness:

1) Compassion—the capacity to show empathy and fellowship.

2) Hope—the ability to see light and possible progress in dark situations.

3) Self-surrender—letting go of what is unessential and unnecessary, especially from the past.

4) Transcendence—the way of transmutation; lifting energy and activity into higher expression—often the process of sublimation, the redirecting of energy into higher faculties of creativity.

5) Forgiveness—letting go of past hurts and loving more, through our own failings and failings of others.

6) Unconditional Love—the unchanging attitude of love and acceptance of others, while not necessarily condoning their behaviors.

7) Magnanimity—great-heartedness in all things; the ability to rise above a situation or limitation.

8) Charity—universal, all-inclusive love and caring.

In creativity, people expressing NINEness tend to seek the other's independent growth and uniqueness. In many ways these people are more married to the world than to just particular partners. They may labor for years unnoticed, then may come suddenly into the world's spotlight, only to recede again into anonymity. Many will love them; few, if any, will know them. They work better *with* organizations than in them. They tune into the essential "pulse" of others. They can see possibilities and open doors for others, but less often can do this for themselves. They rarely see the results of what they started.

People of NINEness usually work better through the Law of attraction—their good comes to them. They don't make "something" happen through personal efforts. These people often get more nurturing from the eternal than from other human beings. Their lives are a continuous challenge to rise, like Prometheus, out of the chains of limitation and disappointment, moving to victory rather than tragedy.

Observing the Spectrum
of NINEness Energy

The progression from EIGHTness to NINEness moves
people from power to surrender. With NINEness many of
the experiences that were previously in our power now
move to places and conditions that are beyond our control. Whereas EIGHTness exerts and often wins, NINE-
ness must often wait, and it gains more through attraction
than by personal effort.

Wherever NINEness is absent, we can observe little
compassion, slow forgiveness, and a limited perspective.
NINEness emphasizes the totality more than the individual, the best outcome for the highest good, not necessarily
what "I" might personally want. NINEness reveals the
essential equality in God of individuals, the sexes, all
races, ages, and cultures. All lives are meaningfully
interconnected.

In the extreme, NINEness releases in people the tendencies of rescuing, playing Savior, and martyring themselves in the name of service. In certain situations people
may help more by helping less; they may communicate
more in their silence, and they may best respond by waiting when they would personally prefer to act. In the mysterious processes of NINEness, people may not always see
what is most closely in front of them. A solution that has
always been available may remain incredibly invisible and
out of reach until the right moment opens.

Perhaps the greatest potential of NINEness lies in the
possibility of mediation and presenting the larger perspectives of each situation.

The Underdeveloped Expression of NINEness (–9)

The person cannot see the good in others or in events.
Pessimism pervades the atmosphere.

Cynicism expects the worst.

A larger perspective is absent.

Limitations are emphasized at the expense of any healing potential.

The person remains judgmental.

Ideals are rarely present in the person's life.

Misfortunes awaken bitterness and hatred.

Generosity of spirit is not expressed.

The person gives only when there is a guaranteed outcome.

An exclusive attitude cares little about others.

Nobody can tell him or her anything.

Comments are too caustic.

Doubt clouds all hopes for the future.

The Balanced Expression of NINEness (9)

Brotherhood and service to mankind are the most important life themes.

Efforts are all-embracing, passionate and exhaustive. The approach is universal.

Mercy accompanies feelings of forgiveness and compassion.

Delays, interferences, and other testings can lead to overcoming at the midnight hour.

The person is a visionary who acts to mediate and protect.

Space is necessary as well as opportunity for freedom of thought.

Redemption arises out of unconditional love.

There is a need to release the past and wait upon God.

Inclusive love and synthesis bring the best solutions.

The person finds ways to sublimate and transmute energies.

Look for the golden thread that connects all lives.

A generosity of spirit is able to give without expecting a return.

"Wear out, become new" (death and rebirth).

The person is able to resonate and empathize with others and their situations.

When all seems lost, there may be sudden interventions of Grace. They may live "on borrowed time."

Serve the totality and don't hold onto anything.

The person may experience many sudden endings and new beginnings.

Many streams converge to produce intensity and many meaningful moments.

Look for the common ground in human experience; live and let live.

"This, too, shall pass."

Build bridges across endless chasms.

Make the best of impossible people and situations.

Learn to work in the midst of distractions.

The Good Samaritan expresses charity to all.

Pay off old debts and harmonize all relationships.

There is a need always to "be bigger."

The person is often able to bring hope where despair is present.

There are feelings of being an eternal wanderer on earth.

The Excessive Expression of NINEness (+9)

The person is too giving and doesn't protect himself or herself.

There is a failure to conserve energy; exhaustion and illness ensue.

The desire is to reach all people.

It is easy to be consumed by others' needs.

The person may try to save others from hurts and lessons.

Surrender must replace the refusal to let go and release
  feelings and situations.
The person becomes too diffused—an iconoclast.
The person expects too much of himself or herself.
Too much feeling for others becomes melodramatic.
There is a tendency to make life a marathon.
The perspective is too global—insufficiently particular.
Involvement can become extreme and fixated.
Tiredness leads to depression and despair.
Looking too far, one may miss important details at hand.
Avoid meddling in others' lives while trying to "mean
  well!"
By feeling into others too far, a person may lose his or her
  own center and feel disconnected.
From absorbing others' vibrations and from inappropriate
  fascinations, the person's life may become filled with
  sensuality and dissipation.
The person is an "easy hit" for spongers and takers.
The person takes on guilt and a distorted sense of respon-
  sibility for others' shortcomings and failures.
If things don't turn out well, morbidity can set in.
Overindulgence spoils others.
The person links to the point of merging.
It is wise to remember one's limits; avoid taking on too
  much. Learn how to say "no."
The person knows how to give love, but does not always
  know how to receive it well.

Case Study in the Energy of NINEness

A good friend of mine exhibits very balanced energies of
NINEness. Mrs. B. was a colleague in a wholistic counseling department. She always demonstrated compassion
and caring for her clients, whom she served as a counselor. Mrs. B. faced many difficult cases, which involved
interfacing with social workers, lawyers, child abuse

workers, teachers and employers. I always admired her courage and the caring that emerged in all her efforts. Even when Mrs. B. was exhausted from other work she had done earlier in the day, she would show up for her cases in late afternoon and evening, often staying late in emergencies, when more time was needed. I know also that Mrs. B. and her husband have been outstanding parents and caretakers for their own children. Mrs. B. is an outstanding marriage-family and career counselor; I have experienced her excellent teaching skills, shared with a variety of ages and ethnic backgrounds. Most of all, I admire Mrs. B.'s ability to speak to the wholeness of every situation: she is able to be a good listener, offering just the appropriate phrases at the most needed times. Her comments and expertise have helped to save many relationships in crucial moments, when one careless or inappropriate word might have proved damaging. Rarely have her efforts been sufficiently appreciated or rewarded, yet this does not really faze Mrs. B., and she really demonstrates balanced NINEness.

Expanding the Energy of NINEness

1) Recall someone who once hurt you. Create your own process in which you are able to forgive and increasingly love that person.

2) Consider how each person and life are a part of you.

3) Notice three good qualities in a person that you do not personally like.

4) Develop a greater appreciation for other cultures— arts, language, religion.

5) Volunteer a certain number of hours a week to a cause you embrace.

6) Visualize the possible overcomings you wish to realize this lifetime.

7) Use meditation and "light work" to protect yourself from invading negativity.

8) Learn how better to release a person or situation that you have held onto for too long.

9) Using a map of the world, visualize healing coming into various troubled areas of our planet.

10) Develop one helpful, networking idea that will promote better brotherhood and understanding.

11) Where in your life do you need to express more compassion?

12) How can you make today more meaningful for someone else?

13) Find ways to help, without rescuing. Release everyone into God's care when you have done your best.

```
2 7 6
9 5 1
4 3 8
```
To
Contact
the
Energies

The one point at which the divine milieu may be born, for each person, at any moment, is not a fixed point in the universe, but a moving center, which we have to follow, like the Magi their star. That star leads each person differently, by a different path, in accord with his or her vocation. But all paths . . . lead always upward.

— *Teilhard de Chardin*

In this final chapter I want to suggest some possible ways in which you can work with the different energies that come through you. I like to consider some of these creative approaches in terms of the following guidelines — resonance, reflection and inner dialogue. When you are interacting with different friends and personalities, notice how different parts of yourself are stirred and emerge. Truly, others "push our buttons." The marvelous mystery of how we vibrate and respond to others' energies may be called resonance. You can see clearly how different you are with various people as you reflect on time spent with others. Right now, consider who, for example, stimulates your THREEness (your sense of joy, beauty, creativity, and artistic expression) or your SIXness (your nurturing side, your feelings of closeness to friends and your sense of community service), or your SEVENness, etc.

It is clear that all the NINE-fold energies, as they are described through number, are potentially powerful and beautifully creative parts of yourself; as deeply as possible, therefore, it is essential to become increasingly familiar with them. If you feel a certain area of yourself is unbalanced, being either too recessed or too extreme, find people who can awaken or harmonize this energy in you through mutual interaction or resonance. Likewise, use inner dialogue with the different parts of yourself, so that all areas in you might have their "say" and work more creatively with each other. With interest and attentiveness, you can learn how to express the best of your patterns; work willingly and creatively with your weaknesses, and eventually they may become some of your greatest strengths. Avoid denying or fixating; diversify your life; be flexible and sensitive to the larger totality that is in you and in your environment; see the different interactions.

Use the NINE energy pathways as a focusing lens for your life's meaning and its movements. What persons, places, activities and opportunities expand your areas of strength? Who may seem to interact with you in ways that make your energy shrink or go dormant? Who is irritating or troublesome to you, and why—in terms of the energies that are going on? What responses or other energies can you use to maximize your intentions and your purpose? Within yourself keep the dialogue flowing: let that part of you that might feel remote or alienated, too dominant, separate, rejected, or unappreciated, be embraced by other energies. These can communicate within you like an inner network and can help a particular area feel more integrated and harmoniously included. In the Appendix, I have described some different parts of yourself being in dialogue. Keep talking, keep sharing, keep the conversation open; keep negotiating and mediating throughout the colorful spectrum that is you and your world. In this way relationships in your life—with yourself and others, can only improve. Using diversity, move toward a common ground of synthesis and understanding that provides a "win-win" for the greatest number.

You can also "picture" your energies: how they are proportioned presently within you, how they work with each other, and how they might begin to exchange relationships with each other, sharing one-on-one, or in groups. Figure 1 on page 172 provides an image: the large circle—the sphere of your own energy field—is like a fertile matrix. It is the soil in which the NINE energies all interact and exist—within you and in all your outer activities. Imagine one such energy field.

The large circle represents the area of a particular individual, and the smaller circles, inside, signify quantities and influence of varied energies that describe Pythagoras' NINE pathways. Evaluating further, it is clear that this person expresses much energy in the area of 8: power, money, possibly business management, etc. The number 4 connecting with 8 is also strong, which is likely to indicate a hard worker, a high achiever and a structured, scheduled approach to life. Number 5 is small and not completely circular, thus indicating possibly a poor relation to body, unhealthy physical habits, temper or inflexibility, perhaps an inability to have fun or take vacations, etc. Certain energies work well with others, such as creativity (3), inner analysis and knowledge (7), work and routine (4), and business (8). Innovative thinking (1) works well but perhaps less frequently with humanitarian concerns (9). It may be very difficult for this person to share intimately or come close in feelings (2), although he may have groups or family in the schedule (6).

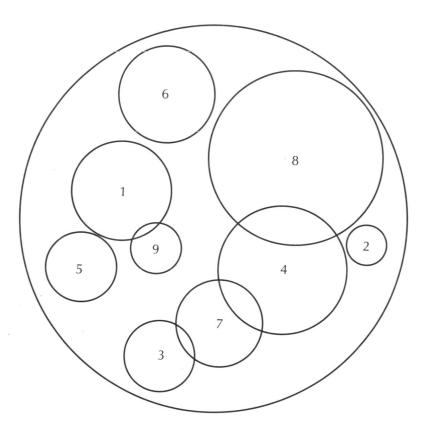

Figure 1. Visual Spectrum Inventory of an individual.

The marvelous human being and teacher John Bradshaw and others have identified three definite stages of
progress: first, identifying and gaining knowledge about a
problem; second, contacting one's feelings about the problem and doing the "pain work" connected with it, including anger and grief; and third, releasing and forgiving,
moving through the healing process and beginning to
move into the new beginnings and areas of life that one

sees for oneself. What do you see for yourself? What are you really here to express? Using the NINE energy pathways and the visual analogy of figure 2 (p. 174), you can write and talk about yourself and your life in the present moment. Use "I . . ." statements, which help you to feel and "own" your expressions of each of the nine energy areas. Again to remind you, the basic themes of the nine pathways can be described as follows:

1) Areas of initiative, capacity to think daringly in new directions, courage and autonomy, ability to verbalize your ideas and thinking, etc.;

2) Areas of close partnership and intimacy; willingness to trust, come close in feelings, be vulnerable, share and be aware of details, facts and the little necessities of life;

3) Areas of creativity and imagination; capacity to feel wonder, to enjoy beauty and nature and to be in love with life;

4) Areas of purposeful activity, planning, work, task completion, goals, scheduling, structure and dependability; excellence in performance;

5) Areas of bodily sensation, flexibility, spontaneity, adaptability to sudden change, adventure, playfulness, and fun, travel and frequent variety, bodily health (sensible diet, exercise, sanitary habits, regular sleep);

6) Areas concerning family, group, community and citizenship; ability to give and receive affection and nurturing; capacity for friendship and social responsibilities;

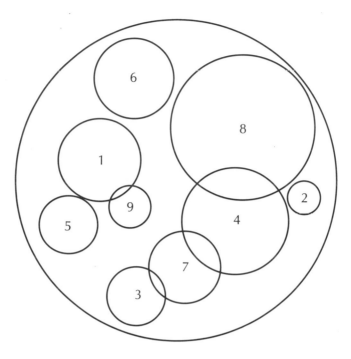

Circle 1: I keep my mind active by _____.
I take new steps in this area: _____.

Circle 2: I feel close to _____ and I show this by _____.
I can improve my relationship with my partner by _____.

Circle 3: I see beauty in _____.
I enjoy _____.

Circle 4: I have these definite goals: _____.
My plan for today is _____.
Today I achieved _____.

Circle 5: I take care of my body by _____.
I have fun when I _____.

Circle 6: I feel _____ about friends, community, etc.
Today, I want to help _____ by _____.

Circle 7: I feel close to the Presence (God) in these ways: _____.
I have knowledge in _____.

Circle 8: I feel _____ about my finances, my position, my ability to take charge, etc.

Circle 9: I help others by _____.

Figure 2. Verbal-Visual Spectrum Inventory.

7) Areas of knowledge, awareness of oneself in God, ability to be connected consciously with the Source of all life, sense of one's deeper direction spiritually; ability to be with oneself—alone and with others;

8) Areas of power, money, authority and management, definable boundaries and limits for oneself and others, ability to lead and take charge, etc.;

9) Areas of brotherhood, service to mankind, compassion and forgiveness, need to release and "close out" effectively, ability to put others' needs before one's own, etc.

Make your own Visual or Visual-Verbal Inventory, filling in your own circle. Be honest as you are taking your inventory of the areas of your life. Notice where the energy of each pathway is "flowing freely" or where it may be blocked, recessed or distorted. If it is difficult for you to talk about certain areas, this is often an indication of a need to release deep feelings, past pain, or angers and frustrations in this part of yourself. As you talk, notice where you might feel certain themes or memories. Where are you carrying the energy in your body? Be sure you are in a safe environment if you find that you are going too deeply into layers of yourself. Take good care of yourself and others as you make your honest evaluations of the different areas of your life. If you feel close and trusting of another person with you, you may even wish to do an inventory of each other, asking for honest and loving feedback as someone else shares feelings about how you are expressing the energies of the nine pathways. (See appendix: Partner to Partner Relationships.)

Where are you this moment in the expression of your energies? Where do you feel blocked or out of touch? What areas are most difficult? What energies do you deeply want to develop further? Where are you the happiest? Pick the single, most important area of your life that you wish to give more energy to. What other persons embody clearly the areas and energies you might wish to express? How can they help or teach you? How might you talk or interact in ways that are mutually most helpful? In a healing atmosphere you will find a setting or environment of wholeness that compassionately accepts all of its parts and in many ways dynamically releases out of the collective power of its own totality. Work toward creating such an accepting, inclusive atmosphere within yourself and in outer relationships. Maintain dialogue; let parts and people keep sharing with each other.

Balance and harmony are rarely expressed in totally equal proportions. Rather, they emerge when we are able to combine effectively many different parts of ourselves. We tend to feel the best when many areas in ourselves are alive and actively being expressed without interfering with each other. A friend of mine once said, "We can remember, Hal, that essentially, there is plenty of room for everyone." Likewise, there is room for the many aspects and patterns of our life, if only we find the ways to express them that are creative and helpful to the totality. If any of these areas are blocked or distorted, our own unconscious will make it clear to us, and if we are receptive, other people will also inform us. Yet all parts are valid and important to the totality. As such, they must find appropriate expression in life.

Try to feel and notice where the energies of your life are expressing themselves. How are they evident in the responses of your physical body, your emotions, your thinking, your intentions and desires? You can view yourself as a mixture of odd and even. Odd energies (ONEness, THREEness, FIVEness, SEVENness and NINEness) tend to break up the usual, more comfortable patterns of your life. They are less concrete or predictable, and require risks into the unknown. They may be felt to be exciting and/or less secure. Even energies (TWOness, FOURness, SIXness and EIGHTness) help to stabilize your life; they tend to bring more outer routine, structure and predictability. Each person is a combination of odd and even. Both aspects of life are necessary. The richer the colors, the more combinations of tones appear. All tones are necessary and contribute to the increasing beauty of the totality.

Try to see and live your life in terms of the larger spectrum and continuum of the NINE energy tones. Observe the different sequences and integrations that may be effective. Where do oddness and evenness combine for a more desirable, total outcome? For example, a certain situation may call for much imagination, creativity and drama (THREEness), while also requiring clear boundaries, decisions and financial management (EIGHTness). Likewise, fun, variety and flexibility (FIVEness) may be even more expansive in the company of clear goals, planning and scheduling (FOURness). It is clear that all the NINE energy streams carry themes and content that can flow together, offering an incredible wealth of rhythms and colors. Call forth these dynamic energy resources to meet the particular challenges of your life. Find the people that can interact most creatively, helpfully and cooperatively to achieve the desired outcome. If difficulties arise in certain areas, use the "bookend approach." Wherever the trouble lies (in a particular pathway), use the pathways on either side as a means of bringing the imbalance into centeredness. If the problem is "odd," the solution is often "even." Identify issues and see where the energy needs to move. Cultivate the opposite, replace and redirect the energy appropriately. Diversify throughout the total spectrum and unify. Let us take a few case histories where we can combine the two approaches of the "bookend" and "full spectrum" treatment.

Mr. M. (3) + 4 - 5

Mr. M. was found to exhibit the +4-5 tendencies: he tended to be a workaholic, he did not appreciate his family and his schedule was very rigid. He rarely took any time out from his tasks and goals.

Since Mr. M. obviously was strong in FOURness—he did his jobs well and had a clear sense of achievement and excellence—to the point of being a fanatic—the treatment focused on the pathways on either side of FOURness—THREEness and FIVEness. A program of treatment involved a new hobby: a painting class for Mr. M., which he resisted as "unproductive" at first, but which he began to enjoy when he could allow himself some leisure. FIVEness allowed him to explore the energies of travel, movement, and variety. He began to go on outings, he went on some nature hikes, and he found new interest in his family. The group had fun for the first time in years. The ultimate change came when Mr. M. began to jog and allowed himself to experience a full body massage. He felt tensions, stored for many years, softening and unwinding inside him. Today, Mr. M. is just as productive, but his life has more balance, and he and his family are enjoying their time together. Mr. M. is just as dependable and organized, but he can also be more spontaneous. Other sides (pathways) of Mr. M. have come alive in his life expression.

Mrs. F. (5) + 6 - 7

The point of difficulty for Mrs. F. lay in her martyrdom to her family. She was tied to her family, to the excessive degree of doing everything for them. During those rare moments when she was alone, Mrs. F. was lost; she did not know who she was apart from her family. In this sense she was excessively "6." The bookend type of therapy for Mrs. F. tried to help her bring out more of her FIVEness and SEVENness. The FIVE pathway helped her bring more variety into her life outside the home. It also offered her ways to give more freedom to herself and her family. If Mrs. F. went out to the movies some nights with friends, her family suddenly "survived," and began to take care of themselves, especially around the house. Mrs. F. also learned some simple techniques for meditation. She eventually began to enjoy looking inward for the first time in her life. She began to ask within herself if she felt good about what the family asked of her. She went back to school for some deeper training in nursing, which she had given up years before for her children. As her family loved her and appreciated her, they were all supportive of these new moves. Mrs. F. felt nurtured and encouraged in her new pursuits. These family "boosts" were important to her extreme SIXness. Today, Mrs. F. is just as close to her family, but she has diversified and diffused some of her energy into a larger life expression. Mrs. F. now is able to understand her family in a larger dimension—as part of who she is and what she is doing, but the family no longer consumes her identity. She also allows her family more space and freedom.

●　　●　　●

By now it is clear that numbers are energies, not merely mathematical quantities. Great energy streams move throughout the universe, and they circulate through our own being, stimulating and inspiring our lives. When our attunement is balanced, all the energies, called number, do their dance with us and in us; we live in a dynamic harmony, where opposites and all tensions can be continuously resolved.

With this book you can sense more clearly the themes and larger possibilities for every life. Energies in our midst, suggested by number, offer every individual more positive, farther reaching opportunities for creative expression on the great spiral leading into infinite reaches of life.

Using all the number energies available to you, in approaches of creative synthesis, may the magnificent panoply of life's wonder and mystery bring you new openings and discovery.

Appendix

As a further means of finding creative ways to use the energy spectrum of Pythagoras, you can use one of four possible inventories. These are ways of evaluating the energies and responses of the people they describe. These evaluations are designed for different types of relationships, and they come under the following headings:

1) Teacher–Student
2) Parent–Child
3) Employer–Employee
4) Partner to Partner Relationships

You can use these creative inventories in whatever ways they might be useful to you. Feel free to vary or expand them, according to your own particular needs. Notice which areas in you need more or less attention.

Finally, as a means of suggesting the inner dialogue among the various energy streams within yourself, I am including some imaginary conversations that could occur between some of these different areas and thematic interfacings. You can use a single, particular energy to talk to another, or you might use a more "chordal" approach, where two streams embrace a third one, or even more orchestrally, you can bring several of the NINE energy streams into play to face a single, perhaps dominant,

vibration that is moving within you. The chief value of
inner dialoguing is the potential for harmonizing the different parts of yourself. It is only through inclusive loving
and negotiating, in ourselves and others, that ultimately
everyone and every part of us play their parts in truth,
compassion and wholeness.

Using the Inventories

In the following inventories, please feel free to add any of
your own comments that might clarify the statements in
your own creative awareness. The number at the end of
each sentence represents keys to the particular energy
pathways that pertain to the statement. You may wish to
evaluate your responses to the statements in your own
special way: for example, No-Yes-Not Sure, or Rarely-
Somewhat-Often-Almost Always. When you have finished with each inventory, your answers will indicate
what energy pathways need attention and enrichment. As
a teacher, for example, you might observe what qualities
in specific pathways you want to cultivate or emphasize
more with specific students.[1] As a parent, you might discover areas in yourself and your child that need more
attention: for example, you may feel you want to play
more with your child (THREEness and FIVEness) or provide more organization (FOURness) in the home environment. As an employer, you can get a clearer picture of
yourself and how you treat employees, as well as finding a
way to evaluate those who work with you or for you. In
your relationships, the Partner-to-Partner Inventory will
present a picture about how you function in relationships
with others. Find how you may be responding today in

---

[1]Teachers and parents, working with children, are referred to the book *Harmonizing the Classroom* by Hal A. Lingerman and Judy Mathes, Vibrant Learning Enterprises, 1680 S. Melrose Dr., Vista, CA, 92083.

the relationship and discover areas in yourself that may be recessed and presently inactive. Do you want to change these patterns of energy? How can you use other energy pathways to modify an area in yourself that may be too dominant or inactive? How can the other person resonate with you more harmoniously? How do your two inventories blend? How can differences be accepted or resolved?

Table 1. Teacher-Student Inventory.

Primary Strengths and Abilities	Comments (pro or con)
He/She is verbally gifted, able to share ideas, possibilities and is an original thinker (1).	
He/She is willing to risk and shows courage of conviction (1).	
He/She is considerate of others' feelings and sensibilities (2).	
He/She shares and brings harmony (2).	
He/She takes time to do something well (2,4).	
He/She has imagination and is highly artistic (3).	
He/She is a dreamer (3).	
He/She is well organized and uses time well (4).	
He/She is a high achiever (4).	
He/She is dependable (4).	
He/She likes to have fun and enjoys life (5).	
He/She uses his/her body often and needs kinetic outlets, such as sports, gymnastics (5).	
He/She is very restless. He/She needs to move around frequently—releases a lot of energy through the body. He/She needs a lot of room and space (5).	

Table 1.   Teacher-Student Inventory (cont.).

Primary Strengths and Abilities	Comments (pro or con)
He/She makes friends easily and is a helper in the classroom (6).	
He/She is a good citizen and cares a lot about others (6).	
He/She is kind to others; he/she treats them like family (6).	
He/She is with others a lot of the time (6).	
He/She is a joiner (6).	
He/She works best alone in quiet (7).	
He/She studies hard and seeks knowledge, especially in unusual areas (7).	
He/She asks many "deep" questions about subjects and life (7).	
He/She seeks meaning in life, and observes carefully (7).	
He/She wants to be in charge and make the decisions (8).	
He/She frequently questions authority and policies (8).	
He/She stands up for justice and fairness (8).	
He/She is very interested in money and business; he/she wants to win (8).	

Table 1.   Teacher-Student Inventory (cont.).

Primary Strengths and Abilities	Comments (pro or con)
He/She uses power to promote well-being (vs. cruelty and revenge) (8).	
He/She shows compassion and forgiveness to all (9).	
He/She is very interested in varied cultures/languages/religions (9).	
He/She feels pain deeply and often helps the underdog (9).	
He/She is especially sensitive to the outcast, alien, homeless, sufferer (9).	
He/She is especially giving, and is often a mediator (9).	

Table 2. Parent-Child Inventory.

Parent or Provider for Child	Suggestions from Others
I am interesting to talk with, and I have many exciting ideas and conversation that I share freely (1).	
I am interested in what my child thinks about many different areas (1).	
I continuously stimulate my child's interests and the desire to learn. I participate when needed (1).	
I am interested even if I don't agree (1).	
I share feelings with my child; we trust each other (2).	
I try to be comforting when sympathy is needed (2).	
I can be vulnerable as well as strong in front of my children (2).	
I am able to show feelings openly (2).	
I tend to details necessary to the well-being of my children (2).	
I show interest and support my child's creative abilities such as music, drama, photography, animals, projects, assembly, plays, books (3).	

Table 2.   Parent-Child Inventory (cont.).

Parent or Provider for Child	Suggestions from Others
I am able to play "pretend" and do not always take my child's comments or responses literally (3).	
I am "there" for my child (4).	
When I say I'll do something, I do it (4).	
I am regular and on time (on schedule) for my child (4).	
I am interested in my child's efforts and work performance (4).	
I try to prepare my child for the practical necessities of life (4).	
I enjoy having fun with my child, and I can be playful (5).	
I show physical affection to my child (5).	
I participate in some sport or hobby with my child (5).	
I can be spontaneous and flexible according to my child's needs (5).	
I feel good just being at home with my child (6).	
I eat regularly with my child and family (6).	
I help to create a warm and friendly environment with family (6).	

Table 2. Parent-Child Inventory (cont.).

Parent or Provider for Child	Suggestions from Others
I talk freely and am interested in the day my child/family had (6).	
I take my child/family on outings such as picnics, the zoo, ball games, cookouts, rides, movies, restaurants (6).	
I am generous (6,8,9).	
I respect my child's need to be alone (7).	
I try to feed my child's thirst for knowledge (7).	
I share freely in talks about life, God, the stars, dinosaurs (7).	
I use my power benevolently in the family (8).	
I am a good provider (financially) for my family (8).	
I am fair and enforce reasonable policies (8).	
I forgive wrongs and try to be compassionate (9).	
I try to mediate and discuss, rather than bossing (9).	
I instill love and understanding for all races and religions and ages (9).	
When I am wrong, I admit it (9).	
I am strong yet gentle (9).	
I use appropriate discipline, especially with myself (8,9).	

Table 3. Employer-Employee Inventory.

For Employer and Employee:	Suggestions for Improvement
I am always open to new and better ways to accomplish what is needed (1).	
I am very verbal and communicate well (1).	
I am willing to take risks in order to improve my output (1).	
I am considerate of the other people's feelings (2).	
I try to respond to the other's needs (2).	
I am particular and thorough in my efforts (2,4).	
I am a good listener (2).	
I keep things interesting and new (3,5,1).	
I tap the creative abilities of others (3).	
I am on time (4).	
You can count on me (4).	
I finish the task and complete the hours (4).	
I plan well (4).	
Others know where I am and what I am doing (4).	
I can have fun on the job (5).	
I take my break when it is time (5).	

Table 3.   Employer-Employee Inventory (cont.).

For Employer and Employee:	Suggestions for Improvement
I have a good sense of humor (5).	
I can handle sudden change well (5).	
My fellow workers are my friends (6).	
I am loyal and enjoy helping (4,6).	
I fit in well with others (6).	
I am approachable (6).	
I am grateful for my job and workers (6).	
I work better alone (7).	
I'm good at intricate assignments (2,7).	
I prefer not to say much, especially while working (7).	
I like work that is meaningful, not just maintenance (7).	
I don't like surprises (4,6,7,8).	
I respect effort and hard work (4,8).	
I don't like those who try "to get away with things" (6,8).	
I will take a shortcut, if the job can still be done well (5,8,9).	
I like to give the orders (1,8).	

Table 3.   Employer-Employee Inventory (cont.).

For Employer and Employee:	Suggestions for Improvement
I do best when I am in control (8).	
I take correction well (3,6,8).	
I am empathetic and caring toward others (9).	
I will stay late if the situation requires it (9).	
I tend to put others' needs ahead of my own (9).	
I will go out of my way for somebody, even if it inconveniences me (9).	
I tend to do things in an unorthodox way (5,9).	
I work better for short, concentrated hours than over the long haul (3,5).	
I can go with a different method or opinion from my own (1,3,5).	
I tend to be critical of myself or of others (2,9).	
I am a good peacemaker (2,9).	
I get things done (4,8).	
I am honest (2,4,7,8,9 and potentially 1–9).	
I tell the truth (1–9).	
I am patient (2).	
I encourage others (6).	

Table 4.   Partner-to-Partner Inventory.

For Both Partners	Additional Comments and Suggestions
You are extremely interesting to talk with (1).	
It is easy for me to talk with you about anything (1,2).	
You often have a new approach to an old problem (1).	
You will try almost anything, if it makes sense (1,4).	
When you want to communicate, you are usually verbal (1,8).	
You have strong convictions (1,4).	
You are a self-starter (1).	
You prefer to follow more than taking the lead (2).	
You are usually cooperative (2).	
You are very sensitive to my needs (2).	
You are usually considerate (2).	
You are a good listener (2).	
You usually do what I want (2).	
You are often a dreamer (3).	
You are often visionary; at times impractical (1,3,7,9).	
You are affectionate and nurturing (5,6).	
You are demanding (1,8).	

Table 4.   Partner-to-Partner Inventory (cont.).

For Both Partners	Additional Comments and Suggestions
You are a free spirit; highly unconventional (5).	
You follow through and do what you say you will do (4).	
I can depend on you (4).	
You are loyal (4).	
You have a temper (5).	
You are quite casual in your habits (5).	
You love variety, adventure and travel (5).	
You rarely do things the same way twice (5).	
You have frequent bursts of energy (1,5).	
You exercise often and pay a lot of attention to bodily needs and pleasures (5).	
You are clean and bathe regularly (4,5).	
You are often critical (2).	
You need a lot of space and freedom in a relationship (5).	
You love to be at home (6).	
You like to have other persons around (6).	
You like to spend time fixing things (2,4).	

Table 4. Partner-to-Partner Inventory (cont.).

For Both Partners	Additional Comments and Suggestions
You are very domestic and like to cook, clean, shop, set the table, do the laundry, arrange furniture, and so on (6).	
You need a lot of time to yourself (7).	
There are many areas you don't discuss (7,8).	
You always want your own way (1,5,8,etc.).	
You are a student of life (7).	
You are quite private in certain areas (7).	
You prefer to handle the money (8).	
You pay bills on time and regularly (8).	
You take care of your possessions (8).	
You are neat (2).	
You care about the world (9).	
You are compassionate (9).	
You relate well with persons of all ages, color, and cultures (9).	
You always have to be right (8).	
You are fun to be around (5).	
You understand me very well (2,7).	

The Inner Dialogue Process
(Sample Conversations)

ONEness speaking with TWOness: "Let's move ahead by coming up with some new ideas and possibilities."

TWOness might respond, "But I'm afraid that the new ideas will be too threatening; what will happen to my security?"

ONEness then may say, "You're right; this idea is too far-out, but maybe we can find a way to risk, while not causing you worry or feelings of being unneeded (abandoned)."

TWOness: "Okay, but I feel we must research this more thoroughly and get all the details first."

FIVEness interfacing with SEVENness: "The privacy and quiet are driving me crazy. I need to get outside and move around more. I want to have some fun and feel excitement."

SEVENness may say, "I need more time apart from you and the chance to reflect and pray quietly."

FIVEness: "But you never go anywhere or do anything; you're always meditating."

SEVENness: "I need my space!"

FIVEness: "Let's go to a quiet lake and go swimming; or to the mountains for a walk in nature."

SEVENness: "I would enjoy that, if you do not rush me or drive too fast."

THREEness and EIGHTness: "I would enjoy going to a movie tonight or to a restaurant for dinner."

EIGHTness: "I must work late at the office, and I don't have any money to spend just now."

THREEness: "There's no joy in your life; just business, and it's just too sterile."

EIGHTness: "I think we should go to the theater, not just another farcical, inane movie."

THREEness: "Pick one, but I also want to go to a lovely restaurant where the food is tasty, and the surroundings are romantic. I like candlelight."

EIGHTness: "The choices are . . . ! Pick the one you like best."

NINEness and SIXness: "Pete just called, and I have to talk to him about his recent job loss. He's suffering a lot, and maybe I can be of help to him. I hate to see him so down."

SIXness: "Your family comes first; Jackie has his Little League game tonight; you never go to see him play."

NINEness: "But Pete is looking bad and had to go to the doctor today."

SIXness: "You know, Bob, everybody comes ahead of us. You should never have gotten married and had a family. You're married to the world and everybody else, not us."

NINEness: "I love my family—I love you! How can I be with you tonight, then maybe later go to see Pete?"

SIXness: "You'll be very tired for work tomorrow if you stay up late."

NINEness: "But Pete needs me, and I feel for him."

FOURness (practicality and dependability) intercedes: "Why don't you just call him tonight?"

• • •

Integration takes place gradually, as each of us learns to identify our opposing tensions and how to mediate among them. Using the NINE energy pathways, we can move into deeper creative sources within us and beyond us. Other people, who embody different concentrations and proportions of these energy streams, activate vibrations in our own energy field, and the experiences of life that come to us awaken us to our capabilities and our needs. A supreme Wisdom moves in us and in our midst, directing our lives and creative receptivity into a greater order and wonder. Our life is a dance, and each moment calls for new, creative responses.

To offer a sense of some of the different integrations each of us is working toward, here are a few described with varied themes:

TWOness and EIGHTness: the person is trying to bring shyness and timidity together with an ability to make decisions and take charge; or perhaps the dominant attitudes of the energy of EIGHTness need to blend and be more gentle and cooperative—more willing to help to empower the other person, who may be too submissive (TWOness).

FIVEness and SIXness: a free spirit may need to learn family and social responsibility; bohemian tendencies find their center in creative service to the community; or, a person who may be too tied to the family and pleasing others may need to strike out alone, meeting new types and having new experiences.

THREEness and FOURness: the integration comes in blending creativity and free flow expression with dependability and the task; a person who may work too long may need to find a hobby.

ONEness and TWOness: an independent nature is learning how to be more patient and yielding to the needs of someone else; or, a person who is too emotionally needy must learn to think through and use creative mental energy to calm the emotions. Risk and safety find their harmony with each other.

SIXness and SEVENness: a type who is deeply bonded to family and group learns how also to think for himself or herself; time alone, apart from others' company, allows inner connections to be made and brings empowerment and meaning to one's life.

SEVENness and NINEness: the quiet inner life, which may be very monastic, is called upon frequently to respond to the needs in the world of many others; solitude and service learn how to work together in the midst of many interferences and sudden interruptions.

Find your own particular integrations. Look for those areas of life and parts of yourself that you may need to balance. Keep the dialogue flowing; see how the energies of certain other people can help you. Being inclusive and selective, discernment grows. Note daily progress.

Life Is . . .

Life is a gift—accept it.
Life is a mystery—unfold it.
Life is a puzzle—solve it.
Life is a song—sing it.
Life is a game—play it.
Life is beauty—praise it.
Life is a promise—fulfill it.
Life is a goal—achieve it.
Life is an opportunity—take it.
Life is an adventure—dare it.
Life is a challenge—meet it.
Life is a duty—perform it.
Life is a struggle—fight it.
Life is sorrow—overcome it.
Life is a tragedy—transcend it.
Life is a comedy—enjoy it.
Life is a journey—complete it.

—Anonymous

Bibliography

Adler, Alfred. *What Life Should Mean To You*. New York: G. P. Putnam's & Sons, 1958.

Anderson, G. L. *Masterpieces of the Orient*. New York: W. W. Norton & Co., 1961.

Arthur, Gavin. *The Circle of Sex*. New Hyde Park, NY: University Books, 1966.

Assagioli, Roberto. *Psychosynthesis*. New York: Viking Press, 1965.

Bach, Richard. *Illusions*. New York: Dell Publishing, 1977.

Balliett, L. Dow. *Nature's Symphony*. Mokelumne Hill, CA: Health Research, 1968.

_____. *Vibration of Numbers*. London: L. N. Fowler, 1905.

Ballou, Robert O., ed. *The Bible of the World*. New York: Viking Press, 1939.

Beattie, Melody. *Codependent No More*. New York: Harper & Row, 1987.

Beecher, Willard and Marguerite. *Beyond Success and Failure*. New York: Pocket Books, 1971.

Belliston, Larry and Marge. *How To Raise a More Creative Child*. Allen, TX: Argus Communications, 1982.

Bloomfield, Harold. *Making Peace with Your Parents*. New York: Random House, 1983.

Blyth, R. H. *Zen in English Literature and Oriental Classics*. New York: E. P. Dutton, 1960.

Bradshaw, John. *Homecoming*. New York: Bantam Books, 1990.

Bullinger, E. W. *Number in Scripture*. London: Lamp Press Ltd., 1952.

Canby, Henry. *Thoreau*. Boston: Houghton-Mifflin Co., 1939.

Bradshaw, John. *Homecoming*. New York: Bantam Books, 1990.

Bullinger, E. W. *Number in Scripture*. London: Lamp Press Ltd., 1952.

Canby, Henry. *Thoreau*. Boston: Houghton-Mifflin Co., 1939.

Capaldi, Nicholas, ed. *Journeys Through Philosophy*. Buffalo: Prometheus Books, 1982.

Cirlot, J. E. *Dictionary of Symbols*. New York: Philosophical Library, 1962.

Cole, K. C. *Sympathetic Vibrations*. New York: Bantam Books, 1985.

Conant, Levi Leonard. *The Number Concept*. New York: MacMillan, 1910.

Curtiss, F. Homer and Harriette. *The Key to the Universe*. New York: E. P. Dutton, 1919.

_____. *The Voice of Isis*. New York: E. P. Dutton, 1919.

Dass, Ram, and Gorman, Paul. *How Can I Help?* New York: Alfred Knopf, 1987.

Davis, John, *Biblical Numerology*. Grand Rapids, MI: Baker Book House, 1978.

de Chardin, Teilhard. *The Divine Milieu*. New York: Harper & Row, 1957.

Erikson, Erik. *Childhood and Society*. New York: Norton & Co., Inc., 1963.

Franklin, Benjamin. *Autobiography*. New York: Signet Classics, 1961.

Frasure, David. *Bluebirds*. Lakemont, GA: Copplehouse Books, 1978.

Fromm, Eric. *The Art of Loving*. New York: Harper & Row, 1956.

Gibson, Walter. *The Science of Numerology*. New York: George Sully & Company, 1927.

Guthrie, Kenneth Sylvan. *The Pythagorean Sourcebook and Library*. Grand Rapids, MI: Phanes Press, 1988.

Hodson, Geoffrey. *The Brotherhood of Angels and Men*. Wheaton, IL: Theosophical Press, 1973.

_____. *The Hidden Wisdom of the Bible*. Vol. 1–4. Wheaton, IL: Quest Books, 1960–1974.

Hopkins, Kenneth, ed. *The Poetry of Railways*. London: Leslie Frewin, 1966.

Johnson, Vera. *The Secrets of Numbers*. New York: Dial Press, 1973.

Jordan, Juno. *Numerology, The Romance of Your Name*. Santa Barbara: J. F. Rowny Press, 1965.

Joy, W. Brugh. *Avalanche*. New York: Ballantine Books, 1990.

Juliano, Arnette. *Treasures of China*. London: Penguin Books, 1981.

Keyes, Laurel. *The Mystery of Sex*. Denver: Gentle Living Publications, 1975.

The Kybalion. Yogi Publication Society. Chicago, IL, 1912.

Lepp, Ignace. *The Ways of Friendship*. New York: Mac-Millan, 1966.

Linthorst, Ann. *A Gift of Love*. New York: Paulist Press, 1979.

Matson, Katinka. *The Psychology Today Omnibook of Personal Development*. New York: William Morrow Publications, 1977.

Mother Teresa. *The Love of Christ*. New York: Harper & Row, 1982.

Murchie, Guy. *The Seven Mysteries of Life*. Boston: Houghton Mifflin Company, 1978.

Myers, Isabel Briggs. *Gifts Differing*. Palo Alto, CA: Consulting Psychologists, Palo Alto Press, 1980.

Naisbitt, John. *Megatrends*. New York: Warner Books, 1982.

Naisbitt, John and Aburdene, Patricia. *Megatrends 2000*. New York: William Morrow & Company, 1990.

Newhouse, Flower A. *The Journey Upward*. Escondido, CA: Christward Ministry, 1978.

Naisbitt, John. *Megatrends*. New York: Warner Books, 1982.

Naisbitt, John and Aburdene, Patricia. *Megatrends 2000*. New York: William Morrow & Company, 1990.

Newhouse, Flower A. *The Journey Upward*. Escondido, CA: Christward Ministry, 1978.

_____. *Disciplines of the Holy Quest*. Escondido, CA: Christward Ministry, 1959.

_____. "Meditation" (taped lecture), January 9, 1955. Escondido, CA: Christward Ministry.

_____. *Quest Lessons*. Escondido, CA: Christward Ministry, 1966.

Oliver, George. *The Pythagorean Triangle*. Minneapolis: Wizards Bookshelf, 1975.

Parrish-Hanna, Carol E. *The Book of Rituals*. Santa Monica, CA: IBS Press, Inc., 1990.

Peck, M. Scott. *The Road Less Traveled*. New York: Touchstone, 1978.

Phillips, David. *Secrets of the Inner Self*. Sydney, Australia: Angus and Robertson Publications, 1980.

Picard, Max. *The World of Silence*. South Bend, IN: Gateway Inc., 1952.

Russell, George, (AE). *The Candle of Vision*. Wheaton, IL: Quest Books, 1965.

Savary, Louis and Berne, Patricia. *Kything: the Art of Spiritual Presence*. New York: Paulist Press, 1988.

Schaef, Anne Wilson. *Co-Dependence*. New York: Perennial Library, 1986.

Scott, Cyril. *The Greater Awareness*. New York: Samuel Weiser, 1981.

Seton, Julia. *Western Symbology*. Chicago: New Publishing Company, 1929.

Spangler, David. *Emergence: Rebirth of the Sacred*. New York: Dell Publishers, 1984.

_____. *Reflections on the Christ*. Forres, Scotland: Findhorn Press, 1978.

_____. *Conversations with John*. Elgin, IL: Lorian Press, 1980.

Taylor, Rodney. *They Shall Not Hurt*. Boulder: Colorado Association University Press, 1989.

Teale, Edwin Way, ed. *The Thoughts of Thoreau*. New York: Dodd, Mead & Co., 1962.

Templeton, Hettie. *Numbers and Their Influence*. Los Angeles: DeVorss & Company, 1940.

Thoreau, Henry David. *Walden*. New York: Dodd & Mead Co., 1946.

Tory, Alan. *Wonder*. New York: Ballantine Publications, 1973.

Trevelyan, George. *A Vision of the Aquarian Age*. Walpole, NH: Stillpoint, 1984.

Uhlein, Gabriele. *Meditations of Hildegard*. Santa Fe: Bear & Company, 1982.

Walton, Roy Page. *Names, Dates, and Numbers*. New York: Edward J. Clode, 1914.

Westcott, W. Wynn. *Numbers*. London, England: Theosophical Publications, 1973.

Whitfield, Charles. *Healing the Child Within*. Deerfield, FL: Health Communications, 1987.

Whittaker, Clio. *An Introduction to Oriental Mythology*. Seacaucus, NJ: Chartwell Books, 1989.

Wilson, Ernest. *Every Good Desire*. New York: Harper & Row, 1973.

_____. *You and the Universe*. San Diego: Harmonial Publishers, 1925.

Hal A. Lingerman is a trained teacher, minister, and psychological counsellor who has worked with various schools, businesses, churches, and other professional groups to help people increase their creativity, understanding of each other, and their basic life intentions. He is a graduate of Drew and Harvard Universities, as well as the Union Theological Seminary and the National University in San Diego, California. He holds Masters degrees in Psychology, Philosophy-Religion, and Russian Languages and Literature. His previously published works include *The Healing Energies of Music, Life Streams,* and *Harmonizing the Classroom.*